"If you are looking for a book that clearly shows how the abused can be restored to new life in Christ, this is it. Jan has shown how Jesus binds up the broken hearted and sets the captives free."

—Dr. Neil T. Anderson
Founder and President Emeritus of Freedom in Christ Ministries
Author, *Who I Am In Christ, Victory Over the Darkness,* and *The Bondage Breaker*

"Too often we carry the guilt of others and they weigh us down and drag us into a life God never intended for us to live. *Set Free* provides hope and healing for those who want to be free from the abuse of evil in all forms."

—Steve Arterburn
Founder and Chairman of NEW LIFE MINISTRIES
Host of *New Life Live!*
Author, *Feeding Your Appetites: Take Control of What's Controlling You!,*
FlashPoints, and *Finding Mr. Right*

"One of every four women in the United States will personally connect with the devastation of abuse reported in *Set Free,* far fewer know the miracle of God's healing. Jan Coates has written an excellent book in which she weaves together the stories, not of survivors, but of 'victors' of sexual and physical violence. *Set Free* has something for everyone: wisdom for church leaders, enlightenment for believers, and soul medicine for victims who have yet to experience total restoration in Jesus Christ."

—Chuck Smith Jr.
Senior Pastor of CAPO BEACH CALVARY CHURCH
Author, *Epiphany: Discover the Delight of God's Word*

"*Set Free* is an important addition to the healing mandate of the church. Too many in our society know the savage devastation, demoralization, and degradation of physical, emotional, and sexual abuse. With boldness and an easy-reading style, *Set Free* presents true stories of survivors who have courageously applied the power of God's healing to their lives. *Set Free* brings light and hope to those whose dreams might have been swallowed by deepening shadows of the past."

—Paul E. Bollwahn, ACSW, CSWM
Lt. Colonel
National Social Services Secretary
THE SALVATION ARMY

"I couldn't put *Set Free* down. Jan has done an excellent job of weaving real life experiences with Scripture. *Set Free* is a must for the abused and those ministering to them."

—Pastor Lorraine Williams
National Chair, PRISON MINISTRY TO WOMEN, OPERATION STARTING LINE
Board Member, PITTSBURGH LEADERSHIP FOUNDATION

"*Set Free* allows you to see and feel God's healing power through the changes he has made in the lives of child abuse survivors. These women have touched the hem of his garment and experienced his healing that is also available to you."

—Florence Littauer
Speaker/Author, *Taking Charge of Your Life, Personality Tree*, and others
Founder of CLASS

"What God has done in Jan's life is what qualifies her to write and speak. She is living testimony that God is a God who loves, forgives, redeems, and restores. *Set Free* is a life-changer for women with hearts broken by childhood abuse."

—Marita Littauer
Speaker/Author, *You've Got What It Takes, Homemade Memories*, and others
Director, CLASS

"Through the pages of *Set Free,* you will discover that faith and hope through Christ Jesus is available to everyone. You will be blessed as you walk alongside brave women who have endured seasons of brokenness, lived out the horrors of abusive childhoods, and experienced deep healing."

—Jeanette Vought, Ph.D., L.P., Lic.S.W., LMFT
Author, *Helping Victims of Sexual Abuse* and *Post Abortion Trauma: Nine Steps to Recovery*
Founder/Director, CHRISTIAN RECOVERY CENTER

"Jan, your book *Set Free* is an echo of so many people's lives that live in hidden devastation. You have captured the very essence of the childhood war that no one talks about, but so many encounter. This book encourages readers to tell their stories—just like the women in the book, to break the vow of secrecy and speak about this unsung war. *Set Free* gently invites the abused to enter God's truth."

—Rev. Joyce Shelton, MA
Pastoral Counselor, Licensed Clinical Christian Therapist
President, WOMEN OF EXCELLENCE MINISTRY, INC.

SET FREE

God's Healing Power for Abuse Survivors *and* Those Who Love Them

JAN COATES

BETHANY HOUSE PUBLISHERS

Minneapolis, Minnesota

Published by Bethany House Publishers
11400 Hampshire Avenue South
Bloomington, Minnesota 55438

Bethany House Publishers is a division of
Baker Publishing Group, Grand Rapids, Michigan.

Printed in the United States of America

Library of Congress Cataloging-in-Publication Data

Coates Jan.
    Set free : God's healing power for abuse survivors—and those who love them / by Jan Coates.
        p. cm.
    Summary: "One in three American women is a survivor of child abuse. This book offers help and encouragement for God's healing and includes resources for women to take 'next steps' in the healing process"—Provided by publisher.
    Includes bibliographical references.
    ISBN 0-7642-0040-2 (pbk.)
    1. Adult child abuse victims—Religious life. 2. Christian women—Religious life. I. Title.
    BV4596.A25 C63 2005
    261.8'3273—dc22
                                                        2005004893

SPECIAL APPRECIATION AND ACKNOWLEDGMENTS

My heavenly Father ignited a fire in me to initiate and complete this book on overcoming child abuse. I'm deeply humbled and thankful that the Lord chose me, a once empty and broken vessel, to pour out to others the love he has poured into me.

Thank you to my husband, Bill, for loving me throughout the birth pangs and the delivery of this special book; thanks also to my son, Matthew, and my daughter, Jordan, for believing in "Mom."

Words cannot express the deep gratitude to my heroes and my sisters in Christ, who bravely walked beside me during the past two years. These courageous, transparent overcomers reveal their souls in this book, reliving the depths of their past child abuses so that other women may find God's unconditional love and healing.

A special thanks to Nanette Thorsen-Snipes for helping me over the editing hurdles and keeping me focused on the finish line.

Twenty-three years ago Pastor Roger Nelson of Lone Jack Baptist Church in Missouri extended love and compassion to this broken vessel. He provided godly wisdom during the depths of my complete brokenness while leading me back to God's family. I didn't want to live, but Roger and the Lord had other plans. Thank you, Roger, for the compassionate healing you administered through Jesus. You're a great example of a servant the Lord uses for the "hard cases."

Warm thanks to all my Bible study groups, prayer warriors,

friends, and church family who believed *Set Free* would be a reality.

Thank you to Marita Littauer and the gang at CLASServices who, over the years, provided their seminars, training, and ongoing encouragement.

Last, but not least, thanks to Janet Kobobel Grant, my agent, and the team at Bethany. Thanks for making it happen.

JAN COATES has worked in sales, marketing, and creative writing for more than twenty-five years. She is a speaker who has appeared on television and radio shows. For more than ten years she owned Creative Design/Marketing Solutions, a sales and marketing consulting company. Jan also served as a founding member of Mothers Against Drunk Drivers (MADD), Kansas City, Missouri Chapter.

Jan publicly accepted Jesus Christ as her Savior at the age of ten, but as a teen, overwhelmed with shame and guilt from a childhood marred with emotional, physical, and sexual abuse, Jan hid from the Lord.

In 1982, when a drunk driver killed Jan's only child, she called out to God in desperation. The Lord responded to her with his love, mercy, and grace—he rescued and redeemed her. Jan publicly rededicated her life to Jesus on Easter Sunday, 1983.

Since that day the Lord has been gradually changing Jan from a broken, hard-hearted victim into a tender overcomer—complete with a new heart and a new spirit.

Today, Jan and her husband, Bill, are the proud parents of two teenagers and live in Texas.

You may contact Jan at:

jan@jancoates.com
www.jancoates.com

CONTENTS

FOREWORD

It's no secret that God loves good-looking, well-behaved suburban American women. They have been held up as role models by the church and Christian media for so long that many people have come to equate Christianity with good-looking, well-behaved suburban American women. That's rather unfortunate, because as the Scripture says, "[God's] power is made perfect in weakness" (2 Corinthians 12:9). By focusing all of our attention on Christians who present the most polished images, the church has been robbed of a blessing. We've failed to see the mind-boggling power of a God who reaches down into the unseemly places—into the ghettos, the abusive homes, the crack houses—to liberate the oppressed and the abused. While churches have kept busy hosting seminars on how to organize your pantry, your money, and your wardrobe, God has been running rescue missions a yard from the gates of hell.

The measure of a woman's life is not where she lives, how she looks, or how well she cooks; the measure of a woman's life is how far she's come by the grace of God. In this book, Jan Coates introduces us to women who have been *Set Free*— many of them from situations so horrible we would rather look away than admit that such abuse takes place. But it's time to face reality. Every day in this country, women and children are being subjected to unspeakable abuse while the church keeps silent. Or worse, offers up simplistic answers that impart more hurt than hope. Believe me, I know. The stories on the pages of this book are my story, too. Maybe they are your story, as well. If so, I believe you will find new hope and confidence as you read these stories of *God's Healing Power for Abuse Survivors*.

It is my prayer that *Set Free* will pull back the curtain on a previously concealed segment of the Body of Christ: women who love much because they've been forgiven and healed of much. These women are an untapped resource, a mighty army waiting to arise. Their hour has come. Fellow survivors, I urge you to come out of the shadows. Read these stories and let them empower you. Let the floodgates of grace and truth be unleashed as women who have been Set Free get up out of the back pew and loudly proclaim the great things God has done.

His Vessel,

Donna Partow
www.donnapartow.com

INTRODUCTION

"For I know the plans I have for you," declares the Lord,
"plans to prosper you and not to harm you, plans to give
you hope and a future."
JEREMIAH 29:11

❖

From creation, God planned for all children to be raised in a godly, healthy environment. Unfortunately, that does not always happen. Every day children are abused, abandoned, and neglected. The effects of this kind of abuse can devastate a child long beyond childhood. I can tell you that from firsthand experience, based on my own terrifying, abusive childhood.

Without our consent, the trauma of past child abuse impacts virtually every aspect of our lives, playing out in emotional instability, addictions, mental disorders, and physical ailments. Over the years, many of us have learned to exist by burying the past, denying it ever happened. We limp through life with the scars of our past concealed from the human eye.

But the only way to experience freedom from the past is to face truth and enter into a healing journey.

Whether we're fifteen or eighty-three, if we've experienced child abuse, the child inside us needs healing. We are all in a distinct season of life—some may be acknowledging the truth about their past for the first time, while others may be sorting out the effects of the abuse. Regardless of where we are, we will find new freedom as we release our pasts and pursue our futures through a personal healing journey with God.

Be assured, God has healed others through life-changing encounters.

In this book I tell the stories of several women who hit bottom, including prostitutes, drug addicts, and alcoholics. I gently weave their victorious healing journeys together with Scripture, real-life application, and prayer, revealing how each woman discovered that God had a better plan for her life.

This book will speak to anyone who has experienced child abuse and desires to:

- Feel worthy to call on God
- Have a peaceful heart
- Leave the past behind
- Create meaningful and lasting love relationships
- Experience healing and wholeness
- Embrace the future with a new and thankful heart
- Start today as a new beginning with a bright future

This book will also help counselors, pastors, friends, and family members comprehend the ramifications of childhood abuse and help those they know who are seeking to begin a journey of victory and healing.

This book is designed for individuals as well as groups. The end of the book has discussion questions as well as appendices that contain resources for personal study as well as group discussion.

- *Discussion Questions* will guide us into Scripture passages while also helping us to reflect on our own lives with honesty and intimacy.
- *Names of God* reveals the Lord's relationship to us while identifying his very nature and character. We'll discover that the names of God convey his promises, relationships, authority, and power while providing a personal way to experience and worship our Savior.

- *Who I Am In Christ* cutout to remind us of our special identity in Christ.
- *What Matters* cutout to keep with us as a reminder that God doesn't care what we did yesterday; his focus is on who we are from this moment forward.
- *Question and Answer Section* provided by Dr. Tim Clinton, President, American Association of Christian Counselors, contains information about the "who, what, where, why, and how" of counseling for abuse survivors.
- *Resource Guide* lists Christian counseling organizations, recovery and support resources, online evangelism and spiritual growth associations, as well as emergency contact information.
- *Steps to Peace With God* presents a Scriptural guide with an invitation to accept Jesus as our Lord and Savior.
- *Facts About Child Abuse in the United States* presents the statistics about this heart-wrenching problem.

This book will also, I hope, draw us all into a personal encounter with God as we meet this One who heals the wounded.

I am living proof that the Lord can miraculously transform what society labels a broken outcast into someone new.

Throughout the pages of this book, I refer to readers as my *friends*, because John 15 tells us to love one another and to share everything we have learned from the Lord. As I sacrifice and surrender details of my life and the lessons of truth found in God's Word, I do so eagerly in the hope that all readers, my friends, may also begin to overcome their own difficult pasts.

I know that God wants to give us hope and a future. He can set us free from our pasts and set us free to pursue our futures.

Let's begin the journey.

CHAPTER ONE

God Chooses the Most Improbable

You did not choose me, but I chose you.
JOHN 15:16A

❖

An unknown author wrote a poem titled "The Chosen Vessel." This poem tells how God searches for a vessel to use. " 'Take me,' cried the gold one, 'I'm shiny and bright, I'm of great value and I do things just right.' " God passes by the gold, silver, brass, crystal, and wooden urns, and chooses the vessel of clay. The poem explains why:

> *Then the master looked down*
> *and saw a vessel of clay.*
> *Empty and broken it helplessly lay.*
> *No hope had the vessel that the master might choose,*
> *To cleanse and make whole, to fill and to use.*
> *"Ah! This is the vessel I've been hoping to find,*
> *I will mend and use it and make it all mine."*

Throughout the pages of this book, women will share their true testimonies and journeys. As helpless children, they were violated, neglected, and abused—physically, emotionally, and sexually. For many, the pain and impact of this abuse was so profound that it shattered every ounce of their identity.

As adults they struggled with criminal behavior, drug addiction, alcoholism, prostitution, psychological disorders, and suicide—common problems among adults who were abused as children. Some chose sexually and physically abusive partners; others chose chemically dependent partners. For all of these women, the child abuse of their past contaminated nearly every aspect of their lives.

For nearly forty years I lived with anger, low self-esteem, anxiety, fear, hopelessness, and depression as I repressed the pain and reality of my childhood, filled with physical, emotional, and sexual abuse. Like most victims, I disassociated from the original cause of my anger and helplessness and found expression in destructive acts against myself and others. I tried to fix everything on my own. I failed miserably.

Completely broken, at the lowest point in my life, I called out to God. The Lord heard my cry and responded to me with his love, mercy, and grace. I'm living proof that *it doesn't matter who we were yesterday, or what we did—it matters that God wants to do something with our lives today.*

God never changes. He is the same yesterday, today, and forever. His plan to save us from our own disaster is permanent and everlasting. Throughout the ages, from 2000 B.C. through today, God continually chooses to heal and transform the most improbable candidates.

The moment we place our faith in Jesus, he reaches down from on high and takes hold of us, remembering our past no more.

Why would God use such improbable women? I believe it is because the Lord wants to make clear that the power lies in him, not in people. And when people observe such drastic change in broken lives, their eyes turn heavenward.

The last stanza of "The Chosen Vessel" reads:

> *Then gently he lifted the vessel of clay.*
> *Mended and cleansed it and filled it that day.*
> *Spoke to it kindly. "There's work you must do,*
> *Just pour out to others as I pour into you."*[1]

Like the chosen clay vessel, the brave women in this book, who have experienced divine healing and gradual transformation, pour out their hearts to us. Their message is simple: we can be mended and then *set free*. As their journeys unfold before us, let's walk alongside them and discover the healing and hope available to all through Jesus.

Now meet some of the improbable women of yesterday.

❁

THE DAUGHTER OF EVIL
Elaine's Story

"Elaine, hide under the bed and don't move," her mother whispered.

Elaine crawled under the bed and peeked out from under the bedspread. In horror, she saw her father drag her mother by the hair from the bedroom. Her mother's screams punctuated the early morning peace. Elaine clapped her hands over her ears to block out the sound. How she wished she could save her mother.

The only escape Elaine found from a brutal father who ran with hoodlums was the TV shows of the '50s, *Father Knows Best* and *Leave It to Beaver*. Only on these shows did Elaine learn about a kinder and gentler world outside the four walls where she lived. She couldn't count the times she dreamed of a dad who loved his family and a mom who was safe in his presence.

She knew the reason the kids at school never invited her to their home to play. The kids talked behind her back, calling her "the daughter of evil." This Deep South community knew her dad well. Word spread quickly about his gambling, stealing, and corruption.

Sadly, everyone from schoolmates to neighbors feared Elaine's dad. One day neighbors watched in disbelief as eleven-year-old Elaine got behind the wheel of their big, fancy car and drove her mother, who had been hit by a bullet, to the hospital. They saw the tragedy playing out in the house many other times, as well, but instead of helping, they hid inside their own houses in fear.

One afternoon a pastor from a community church met Elaine's father, Allen, in the drugstore. The two struck up a polite conversation. Pastor John remembered Allen as one of his basketball students from his coaching days. He had prayed for this troubled young man for many years, even before he heard the rumors all over town.

Just as the two were about to part company, Pastor John asked, "Allen, would you let our church bus pick up Elaine to join us for Vacation Bible School?"

Allen reluctantly agreed, but he told the pastor not to get out of the bus when he picked her up. Making certain the pastor understood the gravity of the situation, Allen cursed, then said, "Don't start that church business with me—ever. Don't ever step foot on my property, and *never* mention God to me. Got it?"

Later, Elaine's father took Elaine and her mother aside and told them what he'd said to the pastor. He pointed a loaded gun at Elaine's head, gritted his teeth, and said, "If you tell one secret at that church, your mother will be dead."

Unfortunately Elaine knew he meant it. He had shot people for much less. Even people who befriended her sometimes disappeared off the face of the earth.

For years Elaine had walked by the pastor's church on her way to the store to get bread and milk. She had peeked into the windows and stared with wonder at the statue of a gentle man wearing a long robe. He stood barefooted with arms outstretched and, curiously, had a ring of thorns sitting on his head.

The day after her father threatened her, wide-eyed Elaine eagerly jumped off the bus and stood right outside the church, gazing at the same statue. Tears slid down her face and she couldn't stop them. Other kids walked by as if they didn't even notice her.

Pastor John quietly waited behind her until she wiped her tears. He whispered to her, "Remember, Elaine, Jesus loves you." She then turned, sniffed, and looked up at him. He gently grasped her hand and they walked through the church doors and into a large room where children were singing.

The words rang out and touched Elaine's heart. "Jesus loves me, this I know, for the Bible tells me so." Years later the words to this song would resonate in Elaine's heart and soul.

❈

THE KEEPER OF SHAMEFUL SECRETS
Liz's Story

Following the divorce of her parents, Liz moved with her mother to a sunny West Coast state, miles away from their small Midwestern hometown. Money was scarce for the family in the '70s, and Liz's mother had to move in with her parents—Liz's grandparents.

While Liz's mother worked at an office, her grandmother cooked and cleaned, leaving her alone with her grandfather.

"Won't you come sit with me and watch television?" Liz's grandfather would say, patting his lap. As a young child, she willingly crawled into his lap, happy to be with her grandfather. What started with cuddling, however, evolved over a few weeks into inappropriate touching. Her grandfather made sure it was in the closed-off den so no one noticed.

Liz became more and more uncomfortable with the unwanted attention her grandfather gave and began refusing to sit with him.

One night as she was being tucked into bed, she tried to tell her mother about her grandfather's inappropriate behavior.

"Mommy," she said, "Grandpa's touching me here."

"Oh, Liz," her mother said, laughing, "you're imagining

things. I don't want to hear you talk like that again."

Over time the abuse worsened. Liz felt truly alone. And dirty. In her heart, she knew what her grandfather did was wrong, but she couldn't stop it.

During those times, her grandfather said, "But you know how much I love you, Liz. This is the way all grandfathers show their love." He'd laugh, then add, "Don't tell our little secret because no one will love you anymore. It would hurt your mother and your grandmother terribly if you told them."

His warning guaranteed Liz's silence, and she was caught in a web of secrecy and deceit, unwillingly playing his game and keeping secrets no child should have to keep. She felt as though she was the "rock" in the family, keeping up the pretense and everyone's spirits while her little-girl innocence plunged further and further below the surface. In order to cope with the abuse, Liz obeyed and kept silent. She simply pretended she lived in a perfect world with a perfect family.

Liz remembers wanting to die—anything to escape the torment. Yet she feared death.

Too young to comprehend, Liz didn't realize that God would do a mighty work in her life.

❦

THE PROSTITUTE
Debi's Story

Debi always felt unwanted. Her mother, an unmarried child from the mountains, lacked the maturity to care for a new baby. As a result, Debi bounced from place to place, living with anyone who would have her. When her mother married and wanted Debi to live with her, Debi felt her life would finally be normal.

For a while Debi's life did seem to change for the better, until the night her mother left her alone with her stepfather. Her mother called to say she would be coming home late, and her stepfather answered the phone.

Debi lay in bed that night, hearing the last of the conversation. She shuddered when her stepfather slammed down the receiver. The door to her bedroom opened, and a crack of light shone across her bed. She closed her eyes, pretending to be asleep.

"Hey, girl," he said, "your mama's not coming home." Debi felt him sit on the bed and heard the anger in his voice. "You're gonna do exactly what I tell you," he said, unbuckling his belt, "or I'll kill you."

Debi inched beneath the covers. She didn't know what he was going to do, but she knew it was bad. He yanked the covers away from her. She remembered screaming and the pain that pulsed through her body. When it was over, she was numb.

He glared at Debi and then got dressed. "Take a shower," he ordered.

Debi slowly did as she was told. The water sprayed over her head and trickled down her body. Her tears mingled with the water and she stifled the sobs that tried to rip from her lips. She felt so dirty, so filthy. She wanted the smell of his sweat off her. What had she done to deserve this? She was only a child. She must have made him mad. He had blackened her eyes several times before and punched her arms, leaving bruises. Yet when she thought about it, she couldn't understand what she'd done to anger him.

What troubled Debi more than angering her stepfather was her mother's reaction. She didn't believe anything Debi said. But maybe that had more to do with the drinking than anything else.

"Mama," Debi would say, "he hurt me."

There were bruises, black eyes, and, of course, the rape, but her mother refused to listen.

"You're no good, Debi," she said. "You're trying to wreck

my marriage, aren't you?'' Her mother poured herself a strong drink and just stared at her.

After a while Debi stopped telling anyone, since no one believed her. The abuse continued for four years. To survive the pain, Debi became numb to everything. She hated her stepfather, her mother, and most of all herself for letting bad things happen.

At age thirteen Debi's mother sent her to her aunt's house where her life resumed some normalcy, except for the words that Satan, the Enemy, whispered in her ear: *You're no good. You're worthless. Nobody loves you.*

Even though her aunt's house was small, it was warm and cozy. Her aunt gave Debi the love she so desired and needed. But the Enemy kept filling her head with lies, which she began to believe. Depressed by the lies and destruction in her life, she rebelled.

Debi's rebellion began with drinking, then turned to drugs—crack and cocaine. In order to continue using drugs, Debi lived on the streets and began selling her body just to survive.

Most of the time, she hid her pain from people, but all around the periphery of her mind it lingered, ready to pounce like a wild animal as soon as something triggered a memory.

One day she decided to hitchhike to another state to see a friend. A compassionate trucker picked her up.

He listened as Debi poured out her problems. Then he spoke gently, fiddling with his sunglasses.

"You know, Debi, Jesus is the answer to your turmoil." He paused before continuing, "You can have peace. Jesus can take away all your pain and suffering. Girl, he can make you a brand-new creation."

Debi stared out the window, trying to look disinterested, but what the trucker said began to plumb the depths of her heart—down in the dark places where she allowed no one.

❀

THE DAUGHTER OF CONDEMNATION
Gayle's Story

Gayle often wondered why she felt worthless, stupid, unattractive, and incompetent.

The nightmare of lies, physical violence, deception, and alcohol began when ten-year-old Gayle stood frozen in fear peering through the crack in her parents' bedroom door.

"Go ahead and hit me!" Gayle's mother shouted. "You're not man enough to do it!" In fear, Gayle watched her military father, dressed in fatigues, standing over her mother with his hand stopped in midair.

Gayle later realized that the verbal and physical disputes directly related to her parents' alcohol abuse.

When her mother divorced her father over his indiscretions with other women, Gayle felt abandoned. She loved both parents, even with their faults.

Gayle's mother became even more dependent upon the alcohol, and through her own unhappiness and bitterness, caused upheaval in a neighbor's marriage. She later married the neighbor, creating more shame and humiliation for Gayle.

Even before her parents' divorce, Gayle lived daily with her mother's verbal abuse; the degrading name-calling got worse after the new marriage.

Gayle's mother habitually called her stupid. Her hurtful words felt like swords slicing deep into Gayle's heart. After hearing her mother shout so many times, "Can't you do anything right, stupid?" Gayle began to believe that she really couldn't do anything right.

Gayle learned to conceal the pain. As if anesthetized, she became insensitive to the emotional and verbal abuse of her mother.

Drinking became her mother's and stepfather's first priority and their only love. Although Gayle was a cheerleader for three years in high school, her mother never saw her cheer.

Over time Gayle began to fill out her dresses and sweaters. Her stepfather noticed the physical changes and became overly friendly.

One evening as Gayle stood at the mirror putting on makeup, her stepfather stood behind her and began to touch her inappropriately. It made Gayle's stomach churn. He made her feel creepy and dirty. Gayle told him to quit; however, the sexual advances continued until she demonstrated her mother's verbal boldness and told him to leave her alone. All she could think of was the day she would walk out the door and never look back.

After high school graduation Gayle left home. Little did she know that she would walk through many doors of life before looking back to the one from her childhood.

❧

The Party Girl
Karissa's Story

Although much of Karissa's childhood is mercifully blocked, she clearly remembers spilling a glass of milk when she was five.

"Get outside," her mother yelled, slamming the door behind Karissa. She held her breath until she heard the click—the familiar sound of the door being locked. She breathed in the sweltering Mississippi humidity. The backyard became her sanctuary where she could swing on the swing set and let the breeze cool her.

Over and over in her mind, Karissa heard—*It's your fault your father left*. Her mother's words chipped at her heart and the swords of anger and bitterness cut her down, destroying her confidence and self-image.

Karissa believed it was her fault that her dad left. After divorcing her mother, Karissa's father married a woman with three sons. "See, I told you!" Karissa's mother would scream.

"Your father never wanted a daughter. He only wanted boys. Just think, if you'd been a boy, you'd still have a father, and I'd still be married."

It must be true, Karissa thought. *Besides, he never calls or writes. He doesn't even remember me on my birthday or Christmas.* What Karissa didn't know was that her mother returned all gifts and cards from her father.

Karissa felt abandoned by her father and unloved by her mother. The guilt sank into her heart like an iron anchor. It weighed her down, making her feel as if she had ruined everyone's life, including her own.

Karissa believed her mother's words, "You'll never amount to anything." Karissa's fear of rejection affected her school performance and social interaction. With every academic, athletic, and social defeat, her self-image spiraled downward.

Despite all of this, Karissa kept herself pure through high school, wanting to save her virginity until marriage; however, that dream was shattered when she was raped at seventeen. After losing the one thing that was her own—her virginity—nothing else seemed to matter. To dull the pain of childhood memories and escape the nightmares of the rape, Karissa turned to drugs and promiscuity.

One night at a party in her friend's West Coast apartment, high on drugs, Karissa listened to a young man talk about heaven and hell. He mentioned evil and darkness filled with a never-ending fire. Karissa could only gasp.

❖

THE HARDENED HEART
Gloria's Story

"God, please help me!" Gloria whispered. "I feel dead inside." She felt as though all life had ebbed from her, leaving her alone in a self-made prison.

She had just returned from burying her twin sister, Gwen.

Her empty arms ached for her, and she felt numb to every-thing. No one could possibly understand what she was going through. She just wanted to curl up in a fetal position and die. Though family and friends stood in her kitchen, she was oblivious to them. From time to time she heard bits and pieces of conversation, but she felt detached.

"Was it suicide or homicide?" a neighbor asked.

"The detective mentioned alcohol and drugs. But it doesn't matter; the answer won't bring Gwen back."

Someone behind her said, "She's survived terrible storms before, but I don't know if she'll make it through this one."

A woman whispered, "Is she responding to anyone?"

Just three months ago Gloria had married Clayton, a solid man who had worked hard to earn her love and trust. Now Gloria sat next to Clayton, wrapped in his warm, strong embrace. The words of the mourners in her kitchen sounded a thousand miles away. Frozen in despair, she continued sinking deeper within her cold prison. She pinched her arm with all her might but could feel no pain. She felt nothing—there was no physical pain and no spiritual pain. She could feel herself slipping away.

As an abused child, Gloria had evaded pain many times. She had learned to live in fear. She had built a thick, protective barrier around her heart to prevent pain from coming in. During those early years, she had frequently prayed the Lord's Prayer for protection with a special emphasis on "deliver me from evil." In Jesus she found security and solace while everything else in her world remained turbulent. She concentrated on how to get out of her evil environment alive.

Before Gwen's death, Gloria had been the leader, the strong one—the one no one could hurt. Gwen paralyzed her pain with alcohol and drugs, limping through life feeling nothing, while surrounding herself with shallow friends and men who used her.

Gloria survived the years of emotional, physical, and sexual abuse, coming away with a hardened heart and a deep inner rage. She suffered silently and tried hard to bury the pain. But like an untreated infected wound, the anger and hardness spread. Over the years, Gloria disguised her deep-rooted shame by overachieving in college, business, and competitive sports activities. To replace her inner feelings of filth, she became a perfectionist, keeping her home spotless and her attire impeccable. She worked eighty-hour weeks, traveling through the revolving doors of major airports while filling her life with business-only associates. Her co-workers called her the "flying tiger." They respected her, but they feared her wrath-filled reputation. Deep down, the child abuse wounds that filled her with shame and unworthiness infected every area of her life.

The pain from losing Gwen ripped through the very fabric of Gloria's life. Every seam in her heart unraveled until she thought she would die.

Then the God she had prayed to as a child spoke to her, not audibly, but through her mind. *Do not fear. Be still, my daughter. I have your heart in mine; I am breathing life into you—be very still, my lost and broken lamb.*

HELP FOR THE HEALING JOURNEY

Each of these women felt helpless, humbled, and broken, with no hope, but God met them right where they were. Some had pretended for years that they were strong enough to make it on their own. Others felt doomed for death or more self-destruction. They all felt they had no place else to turn. It was then, when they reached the lowest point in their lives, that they surrendered in complete desperation and called out to God.

The Lord responded to each of their calls. He rescued them from the depths of disaster and breathed sustaining life into them.

These women, real women whose names have been

changed, will share intimately with us through the pages of this book. We will feel their pain and also their joy as they lay their lives in the hands of the Master Potter. We will also see the broken hearts of these women transformed and *set free.*

We all have two hands. Let us give one to God and one to the survivor whose story appears in each chapter. Let us hold tightly to these hands as we face the past with honesty and a desire to heal. We all need a hand to hold, especially when walking through dark valleys.

When we feel we are in the deepest, darkest, most unreachable area of our lives, we are not alone. God sees us, hears us, and knows our every past experience; he knows what we will experience in the future. The moment we call on the name of Jesus, he reaches down and grasps our hands to lead us through our healing journeys.

Like the clay vessel and the survivors in this book, God chose us. He chose us to be *set free.*

—————————————— PRAYER ——————————————

Father God, I thank you for the brave women who have bared their souls in the previous pages. I thank you that through their stories, I can grasp a hope that can never be taken away from me. I thank you for choosing me, for being with me every moment during my darkest trials. Even when I felt alone and isolated, you were there with me. You felt my pain and you wept with me. Father, I ask that you prepare me to accept your truth as I face it head on. Give me the strength to separate the truth from lies. Release me from the bondages of my past. Father, please hold me steady during the turbulence and guide my every step in accordance with your plans to heal me. In Jesus' name, AMEN.

PART ONE

Recognizing God's Role

CHAPTER TWO

Knowing Truth From Lies

The thief comes only to steal and kill and destroy.
JOHN 10:10A

❀

The lies began to distort Gloria's mind when she experienced the following event with her mentally ill mother:

"My mother yelled, 'Gloria, where are you hiding?'

"I trembled while hiding under the bed. With my back against the floor, I clutched the coiled springs beneath the bed with my hands and feet. I didn't move. I heard the echo of Mother's footsteps leaving the bedroom, and I sighed in relief.

"My thoughts raced. *Jesus, please deliver me from evil.*

"I distinctly heard my mother's returning footsteps. I held my breath so long I felt as though I might suffocate. I closed my eyes, hiding my face in the bedsprings.

"'You are worthless, and I wish you'd never been born!' Mother screeched.

"I watched in horror as Mother hurled a bucket of boiling water at me. My legs caught the brunt of Mother's fury and the burning water.

"I had, once again, wet the sheets, and Mother was furious. I didn't know why I wet the bed every night, and I hated the way it made me smell the next morning.

"I sobbed, 'Mother, I'm sorry. I didn't do it on purpose.' She wouldn't listen."

Today, child psychologists know bed-wetting is a symptom of sexual abuse. Bruises and broken bones also indicate obvious abuse. Other symptoms, however, prove more difficult to discern. Each child acts out differently. Some have nightmares or trouble sleeping. Others experience an abrupt decline in their school performance. Other symptoms may include: poor self-image, inability to love or be loved, lack of trust, depression, fear of certain adults, self-destructive behavior, aggressive tendencies, and anger or rage. The trauma of child abuse is difficult, at best, to pinpoint in a paragraph because child abuse damages the inner depths of the abused.

In the previous chapter, we met women who endured a variety of abusive experiences in their childhoods. Satan deceived these women, penetrating their minds with shame-filled lies about themselves and their position before God. And yet God chose to rescue and transform these most improbable women. His truth set them free from Satan's grip. He can do the same for us. Let's look now at this battle being waged for our hearts.

THE BATTLE FOR THE MIND

"The sexual abuse started when I was six years old," says Gloria. "For some reason, my twin, Gwen, was spared the physical and sexual abuse until several years later. Two separate perpetrators violated me sexually for over five years. One of the perpetrators was my mother's brother. When I told Mother about the incidents, she became enraged and beat me with a metal clothes hanger.

"Later that day I lurked around the living room corner, peeking into the kitchen. Mother sat at the kitchen table alone, gulping a beer while humming, 'When the Saints Go Marching In,' a song we sang at church.

"I said, 'Hey, Mom, you sure hum pretty.'

"'Shush, Gloria,' Mother yelled. 'Get outside and play.'

"I walked into the backyard with my head down, burning with shame and rejection. I dragged my feet in the dirt and stopped to kick a rock over the fence. I looked up at the sky, praying silently, *God, are you mad at me, too? Guess everyone hates me. Why, God, why can't I do anything right?*

Once again Gloria's uncle came to her bed. Gloria knew what her uncle did to her was not right. He was mean to her and he made her feel dirty. Gloria finally confided in her father, a godly man. He held her on his lap, nodding as she spoke. Glancing into his tear-filled blue eyes, Gloria felt relieved that her father believed her. He hugged her with deep compassion, saying, "Gloria, I promise you, that bum will be out of our house soon." Within a few days Gloria's uncle moved from their home while her mother screamed in protest.

When Gloria's uncle moved out, her mother's mental illness worsened. Several weeks later police officers and an ambulance driver forcefully placed Gloria's mother in a straitjacket and removed her from the home. As they took her away she yelled, "Gloria, all this is your fault! You caused this!"

"As a child," says Gloria, "I believed Mother's lies. I felt responsible for the sexual abuse. I believed I deserved the beatings. Worst of all, I lived with the guilt of causing Mother to be hospitalized in a mental institution.

"In my mind I heard over and over my mother's words, 'Gloria, all this is your fault.'

"Consequently, when the second sexual perpetrator began to violate me," says Gloria, "I kept it to myself. Silent, internal pain often manifests itself externally. For me, hives often covered my body, and, again, bedwetting plagued me nightly."

Over the years, it became routine for Gloria's mother to be bound in a straitjacket and taken to a mental hospital.

Raised in a Christian environment during the 1920s depression, Gloria's mother married at fifteen and had her first child by sixteen, triggering an early onset of her mental illness.

"Diagnosed a paranoid schizophrenic, Mother's alcohol addiction intensified her mental illness. Her unpredictable behavior frightened me and everyone who came into contact with her.

"My father tried hard to hold the family together while

continuing to take us to church every Sunday," says Gloria. "He encouraged me to accept Christ as my Savior, which I did at age nine. My twin, Gwen, and I were baptized together. We each received a new Bible and eternal life with Jesus. Several church members who had watched us grow from infants through baptism gave us bookmarks with Scripture.

"I enjoyed church. Most of my teachers made me feel special. They were kind and gentle, making me feel like a different person. I felt clean and lovable on the inside and maybe even pretty on the outside; however, I watched the kids and adults closely, keeping them at a distance so they wouldn't know what I was really like as a person."

Similar to other abused children filled with shame, Gloria feared getting too close to people. She believed if people really knew the truth about her, her family, her mother, and the abuses, that they would not like her.

Shame is not the same as guilt. Guilt stems from our own wrong actions. Shame emerges as a feeling, usually from explicit impressions taught by family members or close associates. We preserve shame internally by treating ourselves the way others treat us. In other words, we live out and believe what others say about us by giving ourselves the same messages. Shame is a lie perpetuated by evil. The lie Satan wants us to believe is that we are the guilty ones. Friends, I'll say it over and over—we are not the guilty ones! We didn't ask for the abuse, and we didn't cause it. It is critical to our health to believe and grasp this important truth.

Gloria says, "I believed with all my heart that Jesus loved me and died on the cross to pay the penalty of my sins. I can't remember not loving Jesus or not believing that he heard my prayers.

"Too young and immature to understand the battle within my mind, I also believed the lies of my abusers—I was unworthy of love, a sex object, a troublemaker, and the root of my family's dysfunction."

One day at school Gloria overheard some of the other third graders giggling and talking about her mother on the kickball field playground. As she walked closer to listen, one boy said, "I heard her mom's behind bars." The conversation muffled while two of the children turned and pointed their index fingers at Gloria. She wanted to run away and hide or curl up in a corner and cry. Instead, she walked up to the boy standing in the front of the small group and kicked him on the shin.

With each passing day Gloria's heart hardened to the comments and responses of others, including her family. Like many abused children, Gloria's past abuses defiled her childlike innocence, slowly changing her into what she labeled an "unlovable child."

"At age twelve I got my hair cut in a ducktail-type style and wore blue jeans with a baggy shirt. In my mind, it didn't matter if anyone liked me because I forced myself not to care. I looked like a boy and assumed the role of a tough girl no one could hurt.

"On Sunday mornings my family assembled, drove to the church parking lot, and rambled into Sunday school. I followed, but quickly maneuvered my way back to the car, where I smoked cigarettes. I didn't want to talk to God—I didn't want him to see that I had turned into a hardened, rebellious girl. In my mind, nothing mattered—not what I did or what I believed."

Gloria listened and believed as Satan whispered over and over, "You're no good. Don't even think about talking to God because he won't give someone like you the time of day."

Beware, friends; words like these create an evil trap filled with lies. Between the pain and anguish, Satan deceives us into thinking we are unworthy of God's love. Satan wants us in bondage (prison) to him.

LIES WE BELIEVE

I don't want to give the Evil One much space, but sometimes we need to remember his existence. Scripture reveals the personal existence of a spirit of evil from Genesis, the first book of the Bible, to Revelation, the last one. God threw the Evil One, Satan, out of heaven because of his sin and wicked ways. His names include: serpent, accuser, dragon, enemy, man of sin, power of darkness, devil, and tempter. His names clearly describe his dark character. Satan is the ruler of the air—he is real, and he has an army of evil followers.

Satan, the thief, desires to destroy the lives of abused children, who, by the sins committed against them, are vulnerable. Satan, our enemy, ambushes us with lies and deceit. He does not rest until he robs us of our worth. He uses our past experiences to place thoughts in our minds, which make us feel rejected and defeated. Satan deceives us into believing we are not worthy to seek Jesus.

The devil does nothing but lie. In fact, Jesus called him the father of lies. Satan's lies especially attack the broken hearts of innocent, abused children. These children, who live with lies and deception, always suffer mentally. Distorted thinking changes their reality, and they have difficultly discerning truth. Most children are not mentally or emotionally equipped to understand the battle Satan wages to win control of their minds. So what is their defense? What is our defense?

Faith defends us against Satan, his flunkies, and his lies. The survivors' stories in the preceding chapter remind us that when we call out to God in surrender and desperation, he rescues us. Our faith stands on the rock-solid promises of God—the truth.

THE REALITY OF TRUE LOVE

The greatest truth the world has ever known is that God loves us. He loves me. He loves all of us. God's love defeats the lies and deceit that try to enslave us. On a human level, we can't understand the love of a holy God—a love so overwhelming that we can only understand it by getting to know him and his character through Jesus. We need to stand for a moment at the foot of his cross and look up.

As God's only Son, Jesus willingly went to the cross so that we, as sinners, may have eternal life by believing that he died, was buried, and arose on the third day, and now sits at the right hand of God. Jesus understands our pain. *Jesus was abused, too.* Jesus suffered humiliation at the hands of the Roman guards. They flogged him with a whip made of sheep bones and lead balls; they spat upon him; they jammed a crown of thorns on his head and forced him to carry his own cross. At Calvary, they drove an iron nail into each hand and through his feet. As Jesus hung on the cross, he bore the sins of all mankind: past, present, and future. Being holy, even God, the Father, for a time could not bear to look upon Jesus as he took our sins upon himself. *Jesus died for us.*

Through the cross, the death of Jesus Christ, and his resurrection, God completely expresses that he loves all of us. God offers us unconditional love and acceptance.

CHOSEN TO BE LOVED

"God is love" (1 John 4:8) speaks of God's character. It tells us he created and designed us to love and be loved. The most important factor in our journey is our love relationship with God. We cannot hide from God, even though we may have tried, nor can we escape him. We must surrender to experience a wholehearted, truth-filled, loving relationship with God. In return for our surrender, we receive unconditional love and eternal life through Jesus.

We may not realize it, but we all yearn to be loved and accepted. We can feel this love from the bottom of our hearts—we are all free to live a life full of joy and love. This freedom means no more bondage to the lies of Satan. It means freedom from the past. It means the liberty to be all Christ designed us to be. That's the freedom Jesus gives us. *The truth will set you free.* When we accept the truth about who Jesus is and trust him as our Savior, his truth sets us free to be who and what we are meant to be.

Consumed with excruciating grief and pain by Gwen's death, Gloria cried, "God, help me." Like Gloria, when we have faith enough to call out to God in our despair, he unites our hearts to his and personal renewal begins.

"I realized God still loved me," says Gloria. "The feelings of unworthiness vanished. In the depths of my pain, I knew God was right there beside me. I recognized his warm, gentle embrace while a quiet calm encompassed my entire being. I could feel new life reviving my broken heart. Yes, I was back in God's arms."

Through his Spirit in our inner being, Christ dwells in our hearts. His Holy Spirit gives us a new desire to love and be loved.

Whether our faith is weak or strong, God loves us. God walked with us during the darkest moments in our abusive childhoods. He walks with us now. He walks with us throughout eternity.

Who we are and what we believe matters to God. It matters so much that his only son, Jesus, died on the cross to free us to love God and accept his love for us. As we reflect on the truth and freedom in this section, let's remember that Christ chose us before the foundation of the world to be holy and without blame before him. He desires to love us as we've never been loved in our lives. He desires to heal us and make us holy before him.

TRUTH SETS US FREE

For months after Gwen's funeral, Pastor Ron gave Gloria words of life—the very words of God, and she pondered every one of them.

"Jesus loves you, Gloria. Enough to die for you on a cross," he said. "For God so loved the world that he gave his one and only Son, that whoever believes in him shall not perish, but have eternal life."

Within six months after losing Gwen, Gloria and her husband, Clayton, accepted a new beginning with Jesus. Together with the guidance of Pastor Ron, Gloria and Clayton began to know Jesus as their personal Savior.

"It makes me shudder," Gloria says, "to think that if I hadn't made that decision when I did, I could be dead now, consumed by the same drugs and alcohol that destroyed Gwen.

"After I prayed to receive Christ in my life, renewing my relationship, I realized that the abuse was not my fault. For the first time in my life, I acknowledged that I did nothing to provoke the abuses imposed on me by my abusers. They owned the responsibility, not me," says Gloria.

Listen to Gloria's words. Read them again. Her words are the first step to the journey of truth that will free us for healing. For years Gloria held on to lies: she deserved the sexual abuses that she endured; she caused her mother's mental illness; she created the dysfunction within her family; her experiences disqualified her from God's love. Satan places these lies in the heads and hearts of child abuse victims. The truth is— the abuse is *never* the fault of the child.

"Then you will know the truth, and the truth will set you free" (John 8:32). Without knowing Jesus, we can't grasp the truth or experience the freedom available to us.

Friends, if you don't personally know Jesus, or if you need renewal, I invite you to receive his love and truth through *Steps to Peace With God,* found in Appendix E at the back of this book.

Gloria's peace with God changed everything about her, including her mind, body, and soul.

"How could anyone love someone as detestable as me? To think that one day I was a bitter, rage-filled woman, and the next day I was saved from the depths of hell by the love of Jesus.

"I realize that during my grieving process for Gwen, I could have continued to believe Satan's lies, staying entrenched in the shame and guilt of my childhood. In my mind, I heard his dark, evil invitation to let drugs and alcohol soothe my pain. I recognized the fierce battle and surrendered to the strong, kind voice of God.

" *'Do not fear. Be still, my lost and broken lamb.'*

"God found me not guilty. I'm no longer unworthy of God's love. I'm free from the past. I have a new identity; I'm a daughter of Christ with a heart that is forever thankful," says Gloria.

No wonder Gloria and the other survivors are filled with a passion that can't be extinguished. God pursued them and loved them first. Their pasts can't be changed, but they've now been *set free* from them. They're ablaze to feel and taste intimacy through a personal and loving relationship with Jesus. Friends, God pursues us until we surrender. Is it time?

—————————— PRAYER ——————————

Father God, I want to have the kind of faith that stands on your rock-solid promises—the truth. I'm worn out from the lies and troubles of my past. I want to be set free. Lord, show me how to surrender my life to you so I can be free to know you, to feel your love, and begin my healing journey. In Jesus' name, AMEN.

CHAPTER THREE

Experiencing God's Power to Heal—Inside Out

I am the Lord, who heals you.
EXODUS 15:26B

❀

Two weeks after she turned twenty-three, Karissa lay in bed alone, sobbing hysterically. Consumed with frantic desperation, she felt as though she had nothing to live for. The shame of casual sex with a co-worker and the side effects of the crystal methamphetamine left her confused and anxious. She submerged deep into a dark pit.

"God, I hate my life. I hate everything about me," she cried. "Am I on my way to hell?"

She recalled a year before talking to a young man about Jesus' second coming. She had listened as he talked of a place where there would be no tears, no sickness, no sorrow, and no pain. Then he mentioned hell filled with evil, the blackness of doom, and a never-ending fire.

Lying on her bed, Karissa began to plead with God. "God, I don't want to die and go to hell." Her eyelids fluttered, and the last words she spoke before dozing off were, "Please let me know I'm going to heaven."

The next morning Karissa took her usual bike ride to the gym. As she pedaled her bike onto the street, a man suddenly opened his car door. She swerved into oncoming traffic and was hit head-on by a truck.

As we discussed in the last chapter, Satan's lies can influence all of us, especially during our moments of vulnerability.

Like many of us, Karissa fell captive to Satan's deception and lies. She was trapped in a web of emotional and mental bondage. Satan and his minions worked overtime to strangle the life out of Karissa, tormenting her already broken heart, luring her into thinking that drugs and alcohol would eliminate her pain. They'll stop at nothing to keep us all from seeking God.

Regardless of what shape our hearts are in, God hears our every prayer, including Karissa's desperate plea for help. God didn't see Karissa as a drug user or a loose woman. He saw her as one of his beautiful children whom he loved, who had been broken and bruised by the sins of abuse.

We all need to hold on to the truth that God loves us unconditionally and forever. Like Karissa, however, sometimes the pieces to our broken hearts lie scattered and fragmented. In this state, our shattered hearts cannot experience the depths of God's unconditional love.

To help us experience God's love and prepare our hearts for his life-changing healing, we must first know him.

KNOWING GOD

God created us to yearn for his love. In God's divine power, beginning with Adam and Eve, he created each of us with an innate desire to know him intimately. God created us with the capacity to know him, love him, and obey him. The traumas of our trials and circumstances can place our quest to know and love God in a state of temporary dormancy; however, our desires to know and experience God last eternally. Some of us may not fully comprehend this passion or understand who God is.

"Who is God?" To answer this, let's look in the Bible, the inspired Word of God, and ask, "Who does God say he is?" Throughout the Old and New Testaments, we find that God has many names, which identify his nature and character. These names will clarify his identity as we press on to understand who God is and why he heals.

Elohim: "God almighty, one true God." It denotes God's supernatural and creative power. Elohim and "El" can be combined with other words to emphasize the attributes of God.

Jehovah: The greatest name of God, meaning "I AM" God, "I AM" Lord. It implies the relationship of God to his creature, man. It comes from the Hebrew verb "YHVH," which means "to be." Jehovah is frequently used with other words to describe the covenant names of God, including:

> **Jehovah-Jireh:** "The Lord sees and provides." The Lord divinely knows every detail of our problems before they happen. God sees our needs and responds with provisions according to his perfect time and will.

> **Jehovah-Nisi:** "The Lord is my miracle," or "the Lord is my banner." When we keep our eyes and hearts centered on him, we will be miraculously victorious.

> **Jehovah-Tsidkenu:** "The Lord is our righteousness." The Lord is perfectly right and just in all that he does and says.

> **Jehovah-Shalom:** Refers to "the Lord of peace." Shalom means perfection, wholeness, and peace. The Lord intends to restore his creation, contaminated by sin, to peace and wholeness.

> **Jehovah-Rapha:** "The Lord who heals you." He is our ultimate healing source—spiritual, physical, emotional, mental, societal, and environmental. When we need any kind of healing, he serves as our Great Physician.[1]

God's names tell us that he is perfect, holy, all-knowing, and ever-present—the beginning and end of all things. The same yesterday, today, and forever, God's love never changes. Rather, his love changes us, transforming us from the inside out. Who would want to make us holy and lovable? His name is God.

The above names represent only a sampling of the many names of God found in the Bible. Please know God can't be defined in a name or a sentence. Books have been dedicated to in-depth studies of the names and titles of God. Local Christian bookstores, the Web, and church libraries can provide additional resources for us to study the names of God. In the back of this book (Appendix A), I have outlined more of God's titles and names.

WHY GOD HEALS

Let us now focus on one of the names for God—*Jehovah-Rapha*. *Jehovah* means "our Lord," and *Rapha* means "to cure, heal, repair, mend, restore to health." God heals, but for many of us wounded by the past, we may struggle to believe this. Why would God heal us?

1. **God heals because he loves us.** God created us for his infinite love. He created man from the dust of the ground and breathed into his nostrils the breath of life, and man became a living soul. God gave us a body, mind, and soul. He desires to permeate every ounce of our essence, even our broken hearts, with his love. In Jeremiah 31:3 God says to us, "I have loved you with an everlasting love; I have drawn you with loving-kindness." We can always count on God to give of himself to meet our every need, regardless of our circumstance.

2. **God heals in response to his promises.** The Bible contains hundreds of verses describing God's healing promises. In Jeremiah 30:17a God says to us, " 'I will restore you to health and heal your wounds,' declares the Lord." Think about it: Jesus dedicated much of his ministry to healing diseased bodies and broken hearts.

3. **God heals because we demonstrate faith.** The Bible tells us in Matthew 9:22 of a woman who had been hemorrhaging for twelve years. As Jesus walked by, she reached out and touched the hem of his garment. Jesus felt the woman's touch and turned toward her. He looked at her and said, "Take heart, daughter, your faith has healed you." By faith, she was healed instantly.

   Throughout the Bible, God heals in response to faith. Faith in God's healing means we believe God has the power and the desire to heal us.

4. **God heals us to bring us to himself.** David the Psalmist wrote, "Praise the Lord, O my soul, and forget not all his benefits—who forgives all your sins and heals all your diseases, who redeems your life from the pit and crowns you with love and compassion" (Psalm 103:2–4). David thanks God for giving us healing, forgiveness, redemption from death, love, and compassion. We accept these same gifts without deserving any of them.

   To be divinely healed means to surrender to God.

EXPERIENCING GOD'S FAITHFULNESS

The faithfulness of the Lord endures forever.
PSALM 117:2B

In an instant Karissa watched as her life unraveled before her.

Karissa says, "I remember lying in a hospital bed and hearing a nurse say, 'She has tire tracks across her chest.' My brother, a paramedic, understood the inference. He immediately contacted my mother, father, and sister, who took the first flight to Los Angeles.

"When I opened my eyes later and saw my father, I thought, *This must be bad if Dad's here.*

"Tears slipped down my face. I tried to speak but couldn't; I was still connected to a ventilator. I saw the concern in my father's eyes. He seemed to be at a loss for comforting words."

Lying in the hospital bed, laboring for every breath, Karissa looked into her dad's eyes for the first time in seventeen years. Seeing him again revived her painful childhood memories.

Karissa dozed into a deep sleep where the familiar nightmares of her mother's abuse continued to haunt her.

Karissa's mother came into the bedroom Karissa shared with her sister. Fearful, they stopped their chattering and listened obediently. "Go to sleep, girls," her mother said. "No talking. No laughing. No nothing. Just go to sleep."

Karissa and Carol, her sister, each had a twin bed. Neither of the girls had a bedspread or a pillow. Their beds were covered with old sheets and army blankets. Like most grade-school girls, as soon as their mother closed the door, they began to whisper again.

"Look, Carol, it is 11:15 P.M. We've never stayed up this late," said Karissa. Watching their puppy lick Carol on her neck, Karissa began to giggle.

Suddenly Carol said, "Shush. Oh no. She's coming back."

It is not uncommon for an abusive parent to select one child from the family as the victim of his or her rage. Throughout her childhood, Karissa remained the primary target of her mother's violence.

"You march right now to the front door, Karissa," her mother said. Opening the front door, motioning for Karissa to go out, she said, "I'll let you know if and when you can come back in."

Karissa, fully aware of the bars, drug dealers, and prostitutes on the next corner of her street, trembled in horror. For protection, Karissa climbed into the backseat of her mother's sedan, locked the car doors, and gazed out the dark window.

At school that day, Sister Ann had taught her a new prayer. Remembering part of it, she prayed, "Keep me safe, God."

Karissa says, "I woke briefly to hear a nurse say, 'She has ninety-three broken bones.' I wondered, *Why me?*

"Though not audible, I heard God's answer. *'This will work together for good.'*

"I wondered how anything could work for good since my condition was grave.

"With a tear in my mitral heart valve, I had a sudden heart attack. I later learned the surgeon had said, 'Karissa probably won't make it through surgery, but she'll die for certain if we do nothing.'"

Six months after her accident, Karissa left the hospital with a smile on her face and a pig valve in her heart. That very week she heard a pastor read from Romans 8:28: "And we know that in all things God works for the good of those who love him, who have been called according to his purpose."

"I could only marvel at God's faithfulness," said Karissa. "The accident had drawn the family together. What the enemy had tried to use for evil, God was using for good."

HEALING INSIDE OUT

"Recovery was not easy," Karissa says. "No scars showed on my face, but the scars on the rest of my body revealed a battle. I had all ten toes amputated. Although I couldn't skip with my feet, my new heart skipped. For the first time in my life, I felt encouraged by my parents' support."

In time, Karissa restored a relationship with her brother and sister. But her greatest joy was in knowing her father truly cared.

Karissa's story shows that God can turn even the most horrid experiences in our lives into something good for those who love him. Karissa communicated her love and trust of God to him through her precious prayer the evening before she was run over. She surrendered her life to him through that prayer.

And God spared her life, healed her body, and healed the physical and spiritual wounds that scarred her heart.

Indeed, *Jehovah-Rapha,* God our Healer, brings life—and brings it more abundantly.

The damage and scars of child abuse run extremely deep, but not so deep that Jesus cannot heal them. Jesus heals our broken hearts and repairs our deepest wounds. No matter what sins we have committed, no matter how terrible our life may be, God loves us. Let's say it again—God loves us! Our job is to rest in his unfailing love and surrender our hearts to him.

As abuse survivors, we have hope because of God. He heals hearts that place their faith and trust in him—we never need to be afraid again. As we replace our fears with God's unfailing love, we let the healing begin.

———————————— PRAYER ————————————

Father God, my heart is thankful because you first loved me. You have shown me that your names reveal who you are and what you do. By faith, I believe you are who you say you are—the all-knowing, all-powerful, holy and great Creator. I call out to you, Jehovah-Rapha, as I give up my life of suffering and brokenness in order for you to heal and change me. Here I am, Lord, surrendering to your healing hands. In Jesus' name, AMEN.

PART TWO

Releasing the Past

CHAPTER FOUR

Pouring Out Our Hearts to God

*Trust in him at all times, O people; pour out your hearts
to him, for God is our refuge.*
PSALM 62:8

❧

Driving on the highway toward home, Gayle's hands trembled as she grasped the steering wheel. Her forehead beaded with sweat. Though she had a husband and kids at home, she felt no one cared if she lived or died. Tears crowded her vision, but she saw the tractor-trailer kicking up dust as it roared toward her.

She says, "I had a sudden urge to pull in front of a tractor-trailer and hit it head on. In desperation, I pulled off the highway and cried out to God."

In the last chapter, we acknowledged the importance of knowing God and surrendering our hearts to him to initiate our healing journeys. Like Gayle, when we cry out to God, we can know that he will orchestrate the right time, circumstances, and people in our lives to support us while we face the truth about our pasts.

For some of us, this will mean finding a support group, a prayer partner, a counselor, or a mentor to walk beside us during this journey. The Resource Guide (Appendix D) in the back of this book lists groups, Christian counseling, and other help we may need.

Believe me, this is not a journey to travel alone.

WHO DO WE TRUST?

Betrayed and broken, child abuse survivors find it difficult to build relationships based on trust. For me, now as I look back, I see how the continual violation of trust in my life progressively deteriorated my ability to trust. Living with an unpredictable mother, I learned at a young age to discern her rage.

One morning while preparing for my afternoon kindergarten class, I grabbed a jar of peanut butter and two slices of bread to make a sandwich to eat while I walked the three blocks to school. Glancing at the kitchen clock, I counted with my fingers and realized I had two hours before my afternoon class started. Suddenly Mother stomped into the kitchen with a belt in her hand and yelled, "I thought I told you to go to school!"

After the beating, she gave me a quarter and told me to buy some candy on the way to school. In my mind, it was her way of saying she was sorry. I bought a candy bar, eating a few bites before entering the school playground. A large sixth-grade girl with a patrol guard belt and badge walked up to me, saying, "What have you got in your hand?" Before I could respond, she said, "Open up your hand. You've got a candy bar. You know you can't have candy on school grounds."

My red and swollen eyes again filled with tears. I focused my eyes on the pavement and trudged toward the school door. Before entering the door, I glanced back toward the patrol guard. I gaped. The fat girl with authority smacked her lips and licked her fingers while devouring my candy bar. Sure, I knew the rules. Now I also knew I couldn't trust her.

The years of sexual, physical, and emotional abuse did a real number on my ability to trust. Operating in a "no-trust" defensive mode, with faulty inner emotional radar, my inability to trust affected my thoughts, actions, and responses. My inability to trust contaminated everything I did and said. I attempted to change the people around me, my past, myself, and even God.

Needless to say, my determination to change others destroyed numerous relationships. As a rebellious teen, I tried to change my past by forcing a new future. Confronting my wise father, I said, "Dad, I can change Bill. I know I can. Let us get married."

"Jan, there's a big difference between going steady with your high school sweetheart and marriage. It won't work," Dad said. "Bill is so young. He likes to hang out with his buddies. He needs to grow up, get all this out of his system, and go to college."

I married at age seventeen and immediately endeavored to change my immature husband. I gave him the rules of our marriage and he broke them, beginning with drinking with his buddies on the weekends, just like Dad had said. While I worked as a part-time office worker, I also attended a business college. Bill did not share my goals of success and money. Laid back, young, and fun-loving, Bill remained the great joke teller at parties and everyone adored him, except me. After our son, Chris, was born, I demanded change. But I did not succeed.

Try as we may, we can't alter or delete our pasts. We can, however, prevent our pasts from controlling us and our future.

Most of us have difficulty trusting and coming to terms with the truth. We need to remember that we can trust and pour out all the deep hurts in our heart to God. With God, we do not have to fear that he will betray our confidence. First, we must face the truth about our abusive childhood head on and then surrender it to God.

We have learned to live with our past in a victim survival mode. This denial method allows us to push, consciously or subconsciously, the abuse and pain from our memory. Our chief means for surviving our abuse depended on a victim survival mentality. In some cases, we mentally left our body during the abuse. Others relied on dissociation (mental separation of self from the experience), creating false fronts, or a combination of methods.

The problem is that as children we learned to hold the truth inside and live a lie on the outside. We learned to build a wall that separated our minds from the pain in our hearts. We learned to trust no one for fear of more shame or judgment, while the lies and truth became blurred. This kind of living is a no-win situation until we place our faith, trust, and confidence in God. He waits patiently for us to trust him with the true contents of our hearts—never forcing us to act contrary to our will. God always knows what is best for us.

"Trust GOD from the bottom of your heart; don't try to figure out everything on your own. Listen for GOD's voice in everything you do, everywhere you go; he's the one who will keep you on track. Don't assume that you know it all. Run to GOD! Run from evil! Your body will glow with health, your very bones will vibrate with life" Proverbs 3:5–8 (THE MESSAGE).

It's pretty clear—God tells us, shows us, and then invites us to run to him for trust; he promises never to betray or abandon us. We don't have to put up any false fronts. We can put the shame and lies behind us. By faith, we will be healed. By faith, we will discover that God can be trusted with our truths. We begin this trust-building journey by allowing God full access to our hearts, holding back nothing.

ADMIT THE TRUTH

Admitting the truth with "Yes, I was abused, and the abuser stole something from me that I will never get back," is an important step to pouring out our hearts. For some, the memories may be fuzzy or dissociated. For others, a specific event may trigger memories of the past abuse. Whatever the situation, the Lord will, in his time, allow us to recall the memories necessary to face the truth during our healing journeys.

I had never faced the truth about my abusive childhood—not with myself, a pastor, a counselor, or, most important, God. A bold friend urged me to seek counseling, saying, "Jan, if you don't get help, I'm going to get it for you."

Struggling with the decision to seek counseling can be overwhelming. The Question and Answer guide, provided by The American Association of Christian Counselors, in the back of this book (Appendix C) will help with this hard decision.

I took my friend's advice and sought professional counseling. As my counselor asked me questions about my childhood, I wondered what, if anything, my past had to do with my present. But over time, like a jigsaw puzzle, the pieces seemed to fit. I discovered that my former physical aggressiveness stemmed from the physical violence I endured as a child. After my son Chris's death I met with a psychiatrist for over two years. When my mother died I participated in therapy for over three years. Based on my experiences, I strongly encourage all survivors of child abuse to seek counseling of some sort. Through counseling, I acquired the skills to cope with truth. I learned to reason and logically analyze situations while gaining some valuable social skills.

Through God I discovered, "Then you will know the truth, and the truth will set you free" (John 8:32).

With God we are safe with our painful secrets. Not once has God told others what we have communicated with him in confidence—he will never doubt us or betray our trust. God waits on us to present our anger, disappointments, hurts, and desires to him. Look at it this way: God already knows the truth, but his healing process encourages us to admit the truth to him so we can acknowledge the damage of our past abuse.

Admitting truth may also include journaling our experiences, counseling, prayer, and/or support groups.

ACKNOWLEDGE THE DAMAGE

Gayle recognized the pain caused by her mother's verbal and emotional abuse as well as the molestation of her stepfather. But like some of us, without a support group, a counselor, or personal trust in Jesus, Gayle tried to escape the pain of truth by evading the problem any way she could. She chose to marry a boy from high school.

It is interesting to note that, with the exception of Karissa, all the survivors featured in this book married during their teens. The authors of *Helping Victims of Sexual Abuse* explain this dilemma. "As defense mechanisms take up residence in the adult victim who has not worked through the recovery process, the adult will experience dysfunctional relationships . . . passive dependencies or over-control—and feel defeated in many areas of life."[1]

"Ironically," says Gayle, "the person I married turned into an alcoholic, too. He constantly battered me emotionally by calling me names and making fun of me. I would slip back into feeling like the helpless little girl whose mother belittled her by calling her stupid. Looking back, I felt my childhood of abuse and negligence set me up for this kind of man; this kind of marriage."

When she finally had enough, Gayle decided to leave. That's when her husband pulled the gun on her. Gayle survived a harrowing weekend and eventually moved out with her children.

Years later, after Gayle's former husband committed suicide, she lost it. She couldn't remember anything. She couldn't even concentrate on how to fill out bank deposit slips or put together a simple recipe.

Gayle says, "I couldn't even remember to bring the laundry from one room to another to wash. Names vanished into thin air. I couldn't understand why, but at one point, suicide even entered my mind. I knew I needed help."

When Gayle first started counseling, she couldn't believe it when the counselor told her that Jesus loved her unconditionally—more than any human could possibly love her. And unlike everyone in her past, Jesus would never leave her, never forsake her. Jesus loved her just as she was.

Gayle's counselor also encouraged her to journal her expe-

riences and feelings, realizing that sometimes it is easier for us
to write memories rather than talk about them.

Gayle chose to journal in the form of letters to God. She
poured out her childhood experiences to God—what happened to her and how it made her feel. Here's a page from
Gayle's journal:

> *Father in Heaven,*
>
> *The counselor brought the pain out from the depths of me. She
> suggested I write you this letter to help me admit the truth of my
> childhood abuses and acknowledge the damage.*
>
> *Father, the worst pain—the pain that made me want to curl
> into a ball—was from Mama. When she drank, she became mean.
> She always said Daddy was self-centered, but Lord, she was, too.
> She became so stuck on herself that no one else mattered, not even
> me.*
>
> *Remember when my teeth got so bad? There were cavities even
> in my front teeth. I was only about eight or nine, and I was
> afraid to smile. I asked Mama to please have them fixed, but
> Mama couldn't be bothered. She said they didn't have enough
> money, but Lord, they could always buy their booze. That really
> hurt me. It seemed everything was more important than I was.*
>
> *I rarely had the opportunity to express an opinion, and when
> I did I was yelled at. So I kept practically everything inside. I
> never said anything to my parents, and I didn't share with others.
> It was just between you and me, Lord. As a fear-filled child, I
> wanted desperately to hear your voice, but I didn't. Maybe you
> were there. Maybe I didn't know how to fully trust you or how to
> hear your voice, either.*
>
> *One day I awoke with unbearable pain in one of my teeth. I
> cried all day with it and by the next day the pain became throb-
> bing. After waiting for me to get over it, Mama finally decided I
> needed to see a dentist. By that time, though, the tooth had
> abscessed. I had to take antibiotics, and the dentist pulled the
> tooth.*
>
> *Only then, Lord, did Mama say I needed to have my teeth
> fixed. It took an entire year when I was twelve to fix every one of*

my teeth that had cavities. I don't think one tooth was spared. Father, why did they neglect me like that? Didn't they love me?

Today Gayle accepts the truth, realizing she was an innocent child-abuse victim. She knows she did nothing to deserve the blatant neglect and verbal attacks by her mother. She did nothing to provoke the sexual advances of her stepfather. She did nothing to cause her father to abandon her. These were all lies from Satan.

When we expose Satan's lies to the light of God's truth, God releases us from the prisons of our pasts. We become free to move forward in full confidence of complete restoration as God's healing hand gently leads us through our healing journey.

RESPOND IN PRAYER

Run after mature righteousness—faith, love, peace—joining those who are in honest and serious prayer before God.
2 TIMOTHY 2:22 THE MESSAGE

"After the divorce," says Gayle, "I moved away and made a comfortable life. But soon the impending death of my mother brought me home again.

"When I first saw her in the hospital, I couldn't believe what the cancer had done. Mama was a shell of her former self, and my heart went out to her.

"I asked Mama if she would like something to drink. Then I looked at the bottle of soda on the table and the two plastic cups. All at once I felt like I was nine years old again. Which one did Mama want? Could I ever do anything right?

"Finally I made a decision and poured the drink.

"The same contempt for me once more spewed from Mama's mouth. 'Not that one, stupid!' she said through clenched teeth. I ran from the room in tears."

Two weeks passed and her mother weakened even further. Gayle knew she didn't have much longer to live. She recognized that her mother had hurt her deeply, but she also knew that she wanted so much to make peace with her mother. So she sat with her, day after day, reading the Bible and praying. She poured out her heart to God, telling him about her pain from her past and now her ache for making peace with her dying mother.

"One evening I sat unseen in the shadows when a nurse came in and gently brushed hair away from my mother's face. She then held my mother's face in her hands. Gently she leaned down and did the thing I could not. The nurse kissed my mother on the forehead.

"The next day the morphine was increased, and I watched my mother's eyes slowly glaze over. I feared I had waited too long to make peace with her. Slowly I walked over to my mother's side and whispered, 'Mama, I'm here. I love you, Mama.'

"My mother smiled, then once again fell under the spell of morphine. I felt the presence of God around me, and it was as though a weight had been lifted. God had heard my prayers."

Through prayer, which is simple conversation with God, we can tell him exactly what we feel. We can pour out our abuse experiences and tell him about our hurts. That may mean we cry, shout, or even moan. Regardless of the method, God wants us to pour out to him the truths about the past. Then we can face them honestly as we seek refuge in his love and protection.

Pastor E. M. Bounds wrote, "Only God can move mountains, but faith and prayer move God."[2] How true his words are. Our prayers affirm to God that we fully trust in his goodness. Whenever we pray with hope, we pour out our lives into the hands of God and fully surrender to his love. The more we surrender, the more we heal. The more we heal, the more his love fills us. Most of us have never known this kind of love, and aside from God, we will never know it.

Opening up our hearts to pray allows God to speak to us in ways we never dreamed possible.

This is a difficult process for all of us. But in order to get the pain behind us, we have to face the sorrow through journaling, prayer, and studying Scripture, and allow the process to change us. It feels easier to run from God, but by running we will never heal. I know because I tried running. God kept after me until I fully surrendered every ugly detail. As I learned to pray, Jehovah-Rapha, our healer, took each abuser's sins from my heart, and my hard heart began to soften.

––––––––––––––––– PRAYER –––––––––––––––––

Father God, thank you for allowing me to pour out my heart to you by studying your Word, praying, and journaling. Remind me, Lord, that acknowledging truth doesn't mean resigning; it means truthfully admitting so that I can move on. Thank you for helping me face the truth about my past and releasing me from the bondage of Satan's lies and deceit. Most of all, Father, thank you for loving me so much that you take away my burdens. You have lightened my heart in order that I may receive more of your love. What an awesome God you are. Never have I known this kind of love, but I accept it now. In Jesus' name, AMEN.

CHAPTER FIVE

Searching Our Souls

*Search me, O God, and know my heart; test me and know
my anxious thoughts.*
PSALM 139:23

❀

"Thank you, Lord—the cardiologist said the pig valve in my
heart is working great. But it feels like the truck that hit me
keeps driving over my heart. The doctor said the pain in my
heart was all in my head. Am I going crazy? Something is terribly wrong. Lord, show me. Search my heart," Karissa prayed.

Today's technology allows doctors to perform miraculous
surgeries, including replacing a valve in a physical heart. As
skilled as our medical physicians are today, however, they still
can't detect a spiritually broken heart with their stethoscopes.
In other words, they may say it's all in our heads. But we know
better, don't we?

Isn't it comforting to know that the Lord intimately understands our pain? As we learned in the last chapter, God not
only knows our pain, but he also knows us and what causes our
broken hearts. He knew us before we were created, and he
even numbers the hairs of our heads. He alone offers us a cure.

"For years," Karissa says, "I took control of my heart,
keeping it private, hidden, and out of reach. Over time, abuse,
rejection, and lack of love shattered my spiritual heart."

During grade school, Karissa attended a parochial school
with strict discipline and little compassion. Her arms covered
with bruises, her body tired from the abusive oppression

inflicted by her mother, Karissa found it difficult to concentrate in school.

"Over and over the nun forced me to write the simple multiplication tables. After I had written them five times, she said, 'Karissa, now see if you can pass this test.' The numbers and formulas on the page blurred in my mind. Once again, I flunked the test.

"She said, 'Karissa, are you doing this to make me mad?' I shrugged my shoulders and glanced down at my desk. Frustrated with me, she then forced me to sit in the dark hallway alone for the remainder of the morning. I lived the life of a victim, and the depth of my despair was beyond anything I could imagine."

In her prayer, Karissa asked God to search her heart. When she did this, God patiently began to reveal her brokenness to her one piece at a time. He began with her own wrongdoings against him and others.

GOD'S SPIRITUAL STETHOSCOPE

The Lord placed his spiritual stethoscope on Karissa's heart and found her fear of death—especially her fear of dying and going to hell. The Lord assured her the moment she prayed and surrendered her life to Jesus, accepting him as her Savior, that his word guaranteed her eternal life with him. He also assured her that when her purpose on earth was complete, she would physically die; however, this death is not permanent.

Like all believers, when Karissa physically dies, within a moment God will change her. He will resurrect her and give her a new and glorious body, complete with working parts. She will spend eternity with the Lord in heaven. She will experience no more abuse, no more broken heart, no more death, and no more sorrow. Heaven will exceed Karissa's every dream. For now, though, Karissa has more to do here on this earth.

When God probed further into Karissa's heart, he also

identified her desperate need for his unconditional love.

Karissa slowly read John 3:16 (THE MESSAGE): "This is how much God loved the world: He gave his Son, his one and only Son. And this is why: so that no one need be destroyed; by believing in him, anyone can have a whole and lasting life."

"For the first time in my life," says Karissa, "I realized God actually gave his Son's life for me.

"I continued to search the Scriptures. I read 1 John 1:9: 'If we confess our sins, he is faithful and just and will forgive us our sins and purify us from all unrighteousness.' I sensed my past sins hindered my love relationship with God. Convicted by this Scripture, I wept and prayed, 'Lord, I want to confess all my sins, but I don't know how or where to begin.'"

God has a unique method for each of us in which he unfolds our pasts and helps us see our unconfessed sins. It can happen over a period of years or instantaneously. He chooses the season, knowing when and precisely how to deal with each of us. God used her accident to place Karissa in a season of continual physical and spiritual healing.

"I believed Satan's lies," says Karissa. "I felt unloved by my family and unworthy of God's love. It seems that over time the lies proliferated, making me imprisoned by my sin as well as the sins of others. All this sin polluted every area of my life."

It can't be said enough—the abuses committed against us, whether verbal, emotional, physical, or sexual, are *not* our sins. Those sins belong to the perpetrator.

Like many of us, Karissa ran away from God. However, Satan deceived Karissa into thinking that if her mother didn't love her, neither would God. But in reality God abided with Karissa every moment, waiting for her to call out and open her troubled heart to him.

Let us allow God to put his spiritual stethoscope on our hearts and help us to see the deception we've been living with as well as the sin that lives in our hearts.

God assures us of his strength, help, and victory, saying,

"So do not fear, for I am with you; do not be dismayed, for I am your God. I will strengthen you and help you; I will uphold you with my righteous right hand" (Isaiah 41:10).

EXPOSE THE DECEPTION

"When I was raped, I went into shock and denial. I felt compelled to lie and cover it up," says Karissa. "I said nothing about it to my family, but I felt so dirty and ashamed. I just couldn't face the truth about what happened."

Fearful of more rejection, hurt, and ridicule, Karissa cut off all relationships with close friends. She stuffed the dirty secret of rape inside her heart, placing the guilt alongside the secrets of not being loved by her mother and feeling like an outsider within the confines of her home.

Let's all remind ourselves one more time—God loves us regardless of the sins committed against us or by us.

When Satan tries to deceive us about our worth, we need to take charge and remember what A. W. Tozer says: "If the devil does come to you and whispers that you are no good, don't argue with him. In fact, you may as well admit it, but then remind the devil: 'Regardless of what you say about me, I must tell you how the Lord feels about me. He tells me that I am so valuable to him that he gave Himself for me on the cross!' So, the value is set by the price paid—and, in our case, the price paid was our Lord Himself!"[1]

"Fearing more hurt and abuse, I fastened the latches to my heart," says Karissa. "I relied upon myself rather than the Lord." Without God, her past experiences made her the perfect target for Satan's web of deception complete with distorted thinking, bitterness, anger, distrust, and unforgiveness. Her bondage to sin induced her to betray and hurt family, friends, co-workers, and more.

"A friend at high school helped me get a job at a nearby fast food restaurant," says Karissa. "Initially, I cooked fries and helped in the kitchen. Within a couple of months, the manager promoted me to cashier, where I pocketed the change from orders on a regular basis. When I got caught, I lost my job and my friend."

In California Karissa secured a job as a cashier in a nightclub, where the cash from the register helped to support her life of drugs and alcohol. During this time, Satan pushed and tempted Karissa until she lost touch with her conscience.

Now, after her surgery, Karissa grieved and mourned, realizing she had three choices while confronting her sins: 1. She could deny them; 2. She could admit them and blame others for her actions; or 3. She could confess and repent.

Blaming others for our own actions only allows our sins to fester, like an open wound, while creating more pain without actual healing. What seems like the hard road, accepting responsibility for our own sins, is actually an easier path with great rewards, including restoration of a love relationship with the Lord.

"I desperately wanted to remove the burdens in my heart," says Karissa, "and to embrace the love of my reunited family. One by one, I confessed my sins to the Lord, and with each confession the heaviness on my heart lightened. Through confession and repentance, God removed the sin from my heart and replaced it with his healing love."

Only God offers us his free gift of forgiveness, filled with love and grace. Not only does God forgive, but he also remembers our sins no more. Our hearts are forever wiped clean. We're free, indeed!

Karissa says, "Accepting the Lord's forgiveness is a process that demands faithful endurance. I was filled with guilt because of the drugs, alcohol, sexual promiscuity, and the way I treated others. I reread forgiveness Scriptures, prayed constantly, and met with my pastor. As I repented and released my past to the Lord, the guilt and shame began to fade away. By faith, I fully accept God's forgiveness."

WHAT IS SIN?

As I write these words, I know that I am a hell-deserving sinner. I also know that Christ paid the infinite debt for all of our sins through his death on the cross. Not a day goes by that I don't get down on my knees and thank the Lord for paying a debt he didn't owe, because I owed a debt I couldn't pay.

Scripture tell us that:

- Sin is an offense against God. (Psalm 51:4)
- Sin is a failure to reach God's perfect standard. (Romans 3:23)
- Sin is a failure to obey God's law. (1 John 3:4)
- Sin is a failure to do the good we know we should do. (James 4:17)

When we trust Jesus, God's forgiveness is continual, and he obliterates our pasts. We need God's forgiveness to move forward in our healing journey with removal of the guilt and shame. When it comes to forgiveness, God stands ready with open arms—he knows of no sin too big or too small to forgive.

WHAT IS REPENTANCE?

Repentance always leads a person to say, "I have sinned," and mean it. Repentance means remorse with a change of direction, making a 180-degree turn. Repentance does not mean asking the Lord for forgiveness with the intent to sin again. Repentance means that we acknowledge our sins, regret our sins, and commit to change. Repentance leads us into a lifestyle that cultivates godliness and removes habits that lead us into sin; it requires action and true brokenness.

Scripture demonstrates the critical importance of repentance in order to restore our intimate relationship with the Lord—the companionship that is broken when we sin. Repentance requires an active change of heart. Through forgiveness and repentance, the Holy Spirit begins to create in us the image of Jesus. We become saints who will be made perfect in our eternal life.

Oswald Chambers says, "The entrance into the kingdom of God is through the sharp, sudden pains of repentance colliding with man's respectable 'goodness.' Then the Holy Spirit, who produces these struggles, begins the formation of the Son of God in the person's life. This new life will reveal itself in conscious repentance followed by unconscious holiness, never the other way around. The foundation of Christianity is repentance. Strictly speaking, a person cannot repent when he chooses—repentance is a gift of God. The old Puritans used to pray for 'the gift of tears.' If you ever cease to understand the value of repentance, you allow yourself to remain in sin."[2]

Beginning this process can be difficult for most of us. We may begin repentant confession with prayer, a written letter to God, recounting sins we are aware of, or journaling. As the Holy Spirit continually convicts us of past sins, let's write them down and pray over them. If our hearts are sincere, the Holy Spirit will guide us every step of the way.

RECEIVE DAILY GRACE

Unconfessed sin separates us from a love relationship with God. Repentant confession restores that relationship. I must admit, it takes the grace of God and the power of the Holy Spirit to say, "Lord, against you, you only, have I sinned."

Let's remember that it is for our good that we confess and return to the Lord. We can do this by setting aside a quiet time every day to pray and communicate our repentant confessions and by daily reading God's Word. Scripture helps us establish a strong foundational understanding of God's truth. Scripture prepares us to stand firm in God through good times and bad. Scripture speaks to us, providing love and gentle guidance for a deeper relationship with God. Everything we need to know about life and living can be found in the Bible.

Friends, let's commit to grow in him until our hunger and

thirst for Scripture becomes insatiable. The message I want you to remember about the pathway of freedom is outlined in the acrostic below:

Freedom
Repent
Embrace God
Experience God

A PROSTITUTE FORGIVEN

Luke 7:36–50 speaks of an unnamed, sinful woman, known by the community as a prostitute, who arrives at a house where Jesus is dining with the Pharisees.

This unnamed woman had heard Jesus speak at other times; she had heard him preaching about repentance and turning from sin. When Jesus spoke of heaven and hell, she had listened intently. She believed what Jesus said, and knew her life of sin doomed her to separation from God.

When this unnamed woman, a notorious sinner, a harlot, a prostitute, heard that Jesus would dine at the house of Simon the Pharisee, she went to see him. She found Jesus in the crowd, walked over, and stood behind him. Realizing Jesus could forgive her, her heart swelled with love and gratitude. In repentance, she began to weep.

Her broken heart ached over her many sins, and the tears continued to flow. She then washed Jesus' feet with her tears, wiped them with her hair, and kissed his feet. While kneeling, she opened a little alabaster vial and poured perfume on Jesus' feet.

The woman humbly served Jesus, while Simon, the host of the feast, offered Jesus nothing. Simon didn't even offer the customary washing of Jesus' feet. The woman not only washed Jesus' feet, but she also anointed them with her perfume.

Simon, a Pharisee, displayed shock that Jesus would allow a harlot to touch him. In Jesus' day, Pharisees were careful to not touch sinners. Their false religious laws prohibited them from touching a known prostitute. These people thought all sin, like color dye in water, could contaminate them.

Jesus then told Simon the story of a man who had two debtors. One owed five hundred silver pieces, and the other fifty. Neither could pay, so the man forgave both men of their debt. Jesus asked Simon which of the debtors would love the man more. Simon rightly replied that the one with the largest debt would love the most.

Jesus then made the point to Simon that the woman's many sins had been forgiven—for she loved much. In other words, she showed Jesus how much she loved him. Jesus then turns his back to Simon, faces the woman, and says, "Your sins are forgiven. . . . Your faith has saved you; go in peace" (Luke 7:48, 50).

Think about it for a moment. The relationship between forgiveness, faith, and love is the basis for Jesus' actions in seeking and receiving sinners. Like Karissa and the unnamed woman who washed Jesus' feet, we, by our faith in Jesus, can also know forgiveness of our sins.

Listen to Jesus' words—the battle is over; our burdens are gone. When Jesus says, "Your sins are forgiven. . . . Your faith has saved you; go in peace," he is speaking to us, too.

———————————— PRAYER ————————————

Father God, "*Generous in love—God, give grace! Huge in mercy—wipe out my bad record. Scrub away my guilt, soak out my sins in your laundry. I know how bad I've been; my sins are staring me down.*

"*You're the One I've violated, and you've seen it all, seen the full extent of my evil. You have all the facts before you; whatever you decide about me is fair. . . .*

"*Going through the motions doesn't please you, a flaw-less performance is nothing to you. I learned God-worship when my pride was shattered. Heart-shattered lives ready for love don't for a moment escape God's notice"* (*Psalm 51:1–4, 16–17* THE MESSAGE).

Thank you, Lord, for showing me my heart and soul. In Jesus' name, AMEN.

CHAPTER SIX

Releasing Our Burdens

Cast your cares [burdens] on the Lord
and he will sustain you.
PSALM 55:22A

❖

God wants us to let go of all our burdens, releasing them to him.

As David wrote this psalm, he suffered persecution and betrayal inflicted by a most trusted, intimate friend. Sound familiar?

How would we respond to such a betrayal?

I doubt our first response would be to say, "Don't worry, it's okay to lie to me. Hey, I don't mind if you persecute me. Go ahead, hurt me physically. And while you're at it, stomp on my emotions. I don't really mind." Preposterous! We'd never say these words.

Like David, our first *human* response would be to feel the agony of betrayal. Like a knife in our gut, the pain is deep and intense. Next, we'd feel our jaws tighten, clenching our fists and feeling the throb in our near-white knuckles. Then, we might fume and let off the steam of our emotions and anger.

David realized that the power to forgive this person, at this point in time, did not reside in him; this type of forgiveness power comes only from God.

I can visualize David unclenching his fists, lifting his palms to the sky, and saying, "Lord, if I keep the sins committed against me, Satan will use his venom to destroy me; therefore, I will let go of these burdens against me. I release them to you in order to maintain my right relationship with you."

Over time the horrid offenses committed against us when we were children become heavy burdens, weighing us down like an iron anchor. They fill us with anger, rage, bitterness, and resentment.

These very real emotions allow us to see and recognize the burdens stored in our hearts. Our abusers committed the worst of crimes against us; however, these burdens hurt us, not them. The burdens we carry inside act like a cancer, poisoning our hearts, souls, minds, and attitudes; they contaminate every aspect of our lives. If we leave these burdens to fester inside our hearts, they have the power to destroy our present and future.

We must remember, however, that no burden is too great for God to bear—not our sins or the sins committed against us as innocent children.

In the previous chapter we learned how to accept God's forgiveness for our own sins. Accepting God's forgiveness frees us from our past while preparing us for a new future. We are renewed daily through God's continual forgiveness.

This forgiveness reveals the very basis of our Christianity. For many of us, however, releasing the burdens from our past abusers presents the hardest process of our healing journey. I stumbled frequently during my long, painful release pilgrimage. I couldn't release on my own, and God didn't expect me to. God's supernatural grace, professional counselors, and the support of friends allowed me to survive this painful process. None of us can go it alone.

Friends, I can't stress enough the importance of trained professionals, counselors, support groups, and fellow believers to walk beside us during this process. The Resource Guide in the back of this book (Appendix D) provides support information and assistance.

Release happens at many different levels. For example, a friend who forgets my birthday prompts a simple release on my part. That kind of pain doesn't wound my heart or damage my life. The process we now begin takes place at a much higher level. And it offers us immediate and eternal rewards.

We commence this portion of our journey for our own benefit—this has nothing to do with our offenders. Here in this deep healing valley, God will emblazon us with grace while transforming and setting us free.

To understand God's perspective on release of our burdens, we need to apply Scripture to our circumstances.

What Is Releasing?

Releasing is a conscious decision to give up all anger and resentment; to cancel a debt. We cannot do this on our own; however, we can depend on God to help us. Christ our model died on the cross to cancel our debt while we were still sinners.

Releasing means not seeking revenge. Sometimes the offenses committed against us were so horrid it is all we can do to keep from seeking revenge. Debi wanted to hurt the relative who sexually abused her. Karissa tormented herself for years contemplating how she could cause harm to the man who raped her. Like the rampage of a tornado, the consequences of revenge and turmoil can destroy us. Satan uses our desires for revenge to deceive us and gain entrance into our lives.

God commands us to step back from any thoughts of revenge and leave him in charge of judgment, wrath, and revenge. To demonstrate our love for God, we must trust and obey him, remembering *we can't control what happens to our hearts, but through Christ Jesus we can control our responses.* God will give us the trust and grace to respond in obedience to him through the release process. And he will greet us with peace and love that passes all understanding on the other side of the process.

While we walk through this refining fire, let's remember that releasing our burdens to God is between us and God, not us and the offenders. They may not deserve it or even want it. This release process is for us.

RELEASING TRANSFORMS

"Before I stepped foot on home soil, I gave my life to Jesus there in the cab of a truck with a man I didn't even know. Instead of knowing *about* God, I began to know him as my personal Savior," Debi says.

Debi surrendered completely to the Lord. She allowed friends, family, and her new church acquaintances to support her. With a repentant heart, Debi asked God to forgive her. She accepted God's forgiveness, feeling like a new person. The Lord then shifted her transformation into high gear, bringing new people into her life to minister to her.

Meeting with her new pastor one day, she discovered that in addition to confessing her personal sins, she also needed to release the burdens she harbored in her heart from the sins committed against her.

Listening to her pastor's words, Debi leaned back in her chair and folded her arms. Looking directly into his eyes, she squinted and said, "You mean, Pastor, I'm supposed to release my anger at the man who sexually abused me? Release my rage against my mother for not protecting me? Release my bitterness against the bums who treated me like trash?"

"In God's eyes, Debi, and in mine, those people committed atrocities against you," he said. He picked up his Bible and read, "It is for freedom that Christ has set us free. Stand firm, then, and do not let yourselves be burdened again by a yoke of slavery" (Galatians 5:1).

"Debi," her pastor continued, "this freedom Christ speaks of begins with letting go of your bitterness and anger toward the people who hurt you—it's a process between you and the Lord."

"Oh, I can't do that. You don't understand, Pastor," Debi said.

"No, Debi, I don't," he replied, "but God does. He waits right now for you to open your heart and surrender the sins committed against you."

"I clenched my grip on the abuses of my past and resisted at first. I wanted no part in the lives of those who wounded me. I didn't care what happened to them, but over my dead body would I live the rest of my life imprisoned by them. No way. I wanted freedom from all of them.

"I wanted to experience love," says Debi, "without performance or conditions—the kind of love Jesus offers. My pastor stayed with me, praying for nearly an hour. *Why should I live in more pain than my abusers? Did I really want God's love more than I wanted to hold on to the nightmares of my past?* Finally, by faith alone, I felt safe asking God to help me release my anger at abusers.

"The pastor later introduced me to several strong believers who counseled and assisted me while I began the long road of releasing and letting go.

"What I released was ugly and painful, but I'm a changed woman today. I'm no longer in bondage to the sins of those who hurt me. I almost let their sins destroy me. Today I'm free to live as the woman God designed me to be."

God initiated Debi's divine freedom from her past. During the release process, Debi became a new creature, allowing the Holy Spirit to form Christ's image within her.

"One day I looked in the mirror and what I saw disgusted me. That very day I got rid of the snug, low-cut sweaters and the tight spandex slacks. I changed my hair from an orange-streaked blond to light brown. I wanted the outside of my body to reflect what I felt on the inside. Clean and acceptable," says Debi.

Over time Debi no longer desired drugs and alcohol. Her past behavior became history, and she no longer felt a need to curse. Debi's favorite Scripture speaks of the cleansing from her past: "Therefore, if anyone is in Christ, he is a new creation; the old has gone, the new has come" (2 Corinthians 5:17)!

God has a mission ready for each of us and a plan to make it happen. God's mission for Debi required drastic change and immediate transformation.

God wants to breathe new life into all of our hearts, freeing us with his Spirit. Healing miracles didn't end when Jesus ascended to heaven; God continues to heal surrendered hearts that seek him. Our job includes surrendering every day, every moment to God's will.

Then the painful burdens within our hearts will unfold, sometimes slowly, in accordance with God's timing. We can't rush this process. It's best for us to wait on the Lord and he will orchestrate the details. In the Lord's time, whether today or over a period of years, he will heal *all* the brokenhearted who trust and obey him.

RELEASING HURTS

My own heart, hardened like unplowed ground from years of sexual, emotional, and physical abuse, shattered into hundreds of hard dirt clods when a drunk driver killed Chris.

Many times I wanted to pray, but I didn't know what to say. The best I could do was groan and cry. In the depths of my sorrow and solitude, I surrendered my life to God. After the loss of my only child, I didn't even have the strength to get out of bed. In time God provided the strength so I could put on my shoes. He also gave me the power to make it through the day, carrying me every step of the way. God used circumstances, Scripture, prayer, and fellow believers to help me begin my new journey.

While reading Luke 4 I discovered that Jesus came to earth in human form to set us (the burdened) free. Jesus said, "God's Spirit is on me; he's chosen me to preach the Message of good news to the poor, sent me to announce pardon to prisoners and recovery of sight to the blind, to set the burdened and battered free" (Luke 4:18 THE MESSAGE).

This Scripture assures us that Jesus pardons us from our sins and that he will show us how to release the sins committed against us while giving us a new way to observe and experience life.

After several years of mourning, my relationship with the Lord began to take on new meaning. I sensed signs of spiritual growth. As a member of Mothers Against Drunk Drivers (MADD), I began to reach out to fellow victims who had lost loved ones or whose lives were shattered because of drunk drivers. I felt their grief and knew their sorrows, empathizing with their anguish. Empathy and caring were foreign to me, and I knew this had to be from God. Amazingly, I could feel the power of the Holy Spirit working through me, encouraging me to pray with wounded people in our close-knit support group.

As a renewed Christian with a weak root structure, I couldn't comprehend what growth in Christ or spiritual maturity looked or felt like. My growth didn't come without *growing pains.* While the Lord prepared me for refinement and maturity, the pains began.

As the Holy Spirit began to convict me of past sins, my heart actually ached from both spiritual and physical pain. I had always viewed myself as a *victim* of maltreatment, and I had developed the bad habit of blaming others for my inappropriate behavior and poor decisions. I now experienced excruciating pain in my heart that felt like the Holy Spirit squeezing the truth out of me ounce by ounce.

Images of individuals I had damaged through my lies and deceit burst into my mind. One by one, I confessed my sins to the Lord, and with each confession, the pressure on my heart lightened. I remembered people from long ago with a clear picture of the anguish and havoc I had caused each one.

It took months of guidance and conviction from the Holy Spirit for me to complete this process. When this portion of my healing was complete, I vowed never to let my sins build into mountain size again. From this painful lesson, I learned the importance of confessing and repenting of my sins at least daily and sometimes hourly.

I began to feel a little self-righteous after my massive confession and repentance, until the Holy Spirit reminded me, through the words of sermons and Scripture, of my need to release and forgive others. I chose to ignore the Holy Spirit.

One morning around two in the morning while slumbering deeply, the Lord struck me with such a jolt I thought lightning had hit my bedroom. I could almost hear him saying audibly, "Jan, we need to talk."

I could no longer act as if I didn't hear God. I fell to my knees, releasing my anger at others for sinning against me. Another long list confronted me. This time I grabbed a spiral notebook and began to write each name, carefully listing the offense next to it.

Throughout the next few months, God continued to divulge my grudges and hurts. I had no idea my heart had become so corrupted with bitterness and anger. When I finally felt the Holy Spirit release me, I placed the notebook in the fireplace and burned it.

Many months later the Lord again woke me early in the morning. I got on my knees and began to pray. In my mind, I heard the Lord say, "Jan, let's finish releasing the burdens in your heart."

Shocked, I thought the Lord had me mixed up with someone else. I whispered, "Lord, no. I've already released everything. Look at me, I'm a new person."

"No, Jan, I have waited patiently. You still have huge burdens in your heart. Come, surrender them to me. Let go."

"Father, believe me, we've done this," I pleaded.

The Lord continued, "But, Jan, you need to release your rage at the man who killed Chris. Your massive pain will slowly poison you. Give it to me. Let go of the anger caused by relatives who sexually abused you. Jan, release your anger toward your mother for the physical and emotional abuse you endured as a child. Your rage and anger will destroy you."

Well, this time I thought the Lord had gone too far. He was asking way too much from me. After all, how could I release my anger about such vicious crimes? Besides, none of the individuals involved were remotely remorseful. They had never even uttered a simple "I'm sorry."

RELEASING HEALS

Inner growth experiences always involve struggle and pain. Genesis 32:24–30 tells the story of Jacob wrestling with God from sunset until sunrise. This must have been a long and resolute match until Jacob realized he was in the hands of the One against whom it is futile to struggle; wrestling with God ends only by surrender or death, whichever comes first. Jacob's submission to God became a turning point in molding this man of faith. In the morning, Jacob limped away a new person. Remolded and transformed, Jacob became completely dependent upon his creator.

"No, I won't release them. Absolutely not!"

I felt like Jacob as I wrestled with God. The Lord would not back off—he insisted I surrender my burdens. He disclosed that he could not continue his plans of growth in my life until *we* had successfully passed through this hurdle. He also revealed to me that the current shape of my spirit and heart did not even come close to his plans of holiness for me. He made me realize that I could never love unconditionally or have his abiding peace until I surrendered and released all.

"Lord, I'm not capable of this," I sobbed.

"I am. Surrender it all. I want every burden in your heart released so you can feel the fullness of my love."

I felt as if I needed sedation as God led me to pray for his holiness, cleanness of heart, peace, and unconditional love.

Several hours later I prayed for release from my rage and bitterness.

During this long and painful prayer meeting with the Lord, I sobbed until I could hardly catch my breath. Finally I let go and surrendered.

I awoke the next morning with the sunlight shining through my bedroom window, feeling like a new person. That day I went about my daily routines, feeling exhausted and empty, but free. It's important to note that I didn't pardon my abusers, nor did I excuse their behavior. I did, however, allow the Lord access to my heart by releasing their wrongdoings to him. By doing this, I gave up my claim to retaliation and allowed the Lord to *set free* the burdens in my heart.

I fought hard with the Lord. And like Jacob after wrestling with the Lord, I still limp.

TAKING STEPS TO RELEASE

As we learn to accept the Lord's forgiveness for our own sins, we become more able to accept the truth about our abusive pasts. Through faith and obedience, we begin to see his healing promises materialize over months or perhaps years as we release the burdens in our hearts. God will fulfill his promises to heal our broken hearts as we take the following steps.

1. Ask God to reveal the burdens in our hearts.
2. Acknowledge the sins committed against us.
3. Acknowledge our pain and the anger.
4. Surrender and release the burdens in our hearts to God.

Sample prayer:
    Father God, I confess that _____ (name of person) hurt me when he/she _____ (name of offense). It made me feel _____ (unloved, unworthy, dirty, rejected, etc.).

    Father, you have said that all things are possible through Christ Jesus. I claim this promise and ask that you release me from my anger against _____ (name of person).

Through the power of Christ Jesus, I release my anger against (name of person). I surrender the sin and the pain to you, Lord, right now through this prayer.

In Jesus' name, amen.

Remember, we are doing this for us, not for any offender. As the survivors in this book prayed, God brought to mind long forgotten people and experiences. God will do this with all of us. Let's stay with this process and endure it while remembering that God's reward of love and peace is just on the other side of our pain, waiting for us with new power and freedom.

FINDING FREEDOM IN GOD'S POWER

The Lord wants every part of us to be free to receive his love and abide in him. After we have released our burdens to God, we will begin to experience real freedom—freedom like we have never experienced before.

Psalm 119:32 says, "I run in the path of your commands, for you have set my heart free." This Scripture says it all. Now we can embrace freedom because we've relinquished our own sins and released the sins committed against us. We can now fully experience our right to stand before Jesus in earnest prayer with expectancy and anticipation of full communion with our Heavenly Father. The burdens that created distance between God and us—bitterness, anger, wrath, rage, and revenge—have vanished. Through Jesus, we now possess the fragrance of love, joy, and peace. In Ephesians 3:12 Jesus promises us: "In him and through faith in him we may approach God with freedom and confidence."

Before we close this chapter, let's raise our palms toward the sky, shout with joy, run to Jesus, and then lie at his feet— we are *set free* to become healed survivors and daughters of Christ.

——————————— PRAYER ———————————

Father God, I am without the power or might to release my anger and rage, but through you I now fully surrender and release the burdens in my heart. I give you my anger, hatred, and bitterness. As you take all this rage, Father, I ask that you cleanse me from all pain and anger. Thank you, Father, for showing me the importance of removing any burden that stands in the way of my relationship with you. Through faith I approach you, Father, with the freedom and confidence to embrace your love like never before. I thank you for setting me free to love you and to grow in your love. Lord, I stand before you a new woman with a heart that yearns to claim my identity as your daughter. In Jesus' name, AMEN.

PART THREE

Reviving
the Present

CHAPTER SEVEN

Claiming Our New Identity

Yet to all who received him, to those who believed in his name, he gave the right to become children of God—children born not of natural descent, nor of human decision or a husband's will, but born of God.
JOHN 1:12–13

For years family, friends, and teachers called Elaine the "daughter of evil." As mentioned in chapter one, Elaine's biological father earned his reputation of a gangster. He viciously beat his wife, children, and anyone who got in his way. Elaine saw the evil, she experienced it, and she lived in fear of it. In her heart she felt as though she was, indeed, "a daughter of evil."

Elaine says, "One day men from my father's crowd grabbed me from my swing set. They took me to an abandoned house where several men drank and laughed at me. They tied my hands behind me and seemed to be waiting for something.

" 'This will teach your mother not to mess around with your dad,' one of the men said, then cursed. He belched in my face and his breath reeked of alcohol. 'Girl, you're not even safe in your own backyard.'

"I knew Mama would be hysterical when Dad told her I was most likely kidnapped and lying dead in some ditch. I wanted to pray silently, but an abrasive voice interrupted.

" 'Hey, little girl, your mother thinks you're dead.' The man's penetrating blue eyes seemed cold and hard as steel."

Elaine knew the man was right. Her mother would think the worst—that she was dead.

Like most street-wise kids living with violence on a daily basis, Elaine learned at an early age that in order to survive she had to make safety and security a way of life. She knew better than to make eye contact with the men. She closed her eyes, trying hard not to listen to what they said. But when the cold-as-steel man spoke, Elaine trembled.

"You know, this kid kind of looks like her old man. Let's just hope she's got his guts and spirit," he said.

"My deepest fear was that I would grow up to be like my dad. Many people commented on our family resemblance, and some even said I had his strength. Many times when Dad beat me, I hoped he would kill me. Being dead would be better than growing up to be like him.

"Later, the phone rang and I heard someone say, 'Kid, your dad said your mother has learned her lesson. You can go home now.'

"At the doorway of our house I saw Mama. Her face was bruised and her eyes red from crying."

Sometimes Elaine felt like two persons. One was unwillingly dragged into a dark, horror-filled world—a world she feared she would inherit because of her father. The other met Jesus at Vacation Bible School where she memorized John 3:16 and learned "Jesus Loves Me." Deep down, underneath the fear and terror in her life, Elaine found a glimmer of hope in Jesus.

RECOGNIZING THE BATTLE FOR IDENTITIES

What Elaine experienced is called spiritual warfare. Satan and his evil-filled agents battle constantly over the possession of our hearts. Satan hates our God. He hates Jesus. He hates us. Evil principalities want us to be victims of our past. The last thing they want is for us to victoriously claim our identities as daughters of Christ.

A. W. Tozer sheds light on dealing with spiritual warfare: "The scriptural way to see things is to set the Lord always before us, put Christ in the center of our vision, and if Satan is lurking around he will appear on the margin only and be seen as but a shadow on the edge of the brightness."[1] Friends, always remember we're children of God and forever daughters of Christ.

Elaine's battle—spiritual warfare between Satan and God—intensified one day when she walked into the bathroom and saw her mother vomiting into the toilet.

Her mother, visibly shaken, said, "Elaine, your father is going to go through the roof. I'm pregnant. You'll have to sleep over at your friend's tonight so I can tell him."

"I felt wanted and safe at my friend's house. They always prayed before supper, and her father always ended his prayer 'In Jesus' name.' I liked that.

"The next morning my friend's mother awakened me. 'Elaine, something terrible has happened. Your mother is in the hospital. Get dressed and I'll drive you over there.'

"When I entered the hospital room I saw Pastor John praying beside her bed. My grandmother held her hand.

"'Is my mommy dead?' I asked.

"'No, but she's in bad shape,' said Pastor John. 'Let's pray for her.'

"I couldn't pray. I just sobbed. Grandma and Pastor John prayed through the day, never leaving Mama's bedside.

"On the way home with Grandma, I silently thanked Jesus because Mama was still alive.

"Grandma spoke softly as she drove. 'Honey, last night your mother fought fiercely for her life. We don't know all the details yet, but your dad was killed.'

"I felt empty inside. I stared at the windshield and, once more, saw in my mind the statue of Jesus. It was the same statue that stood in the church window where I once attended

Vacation Bible School with Pastor John. I felt safe thinking of Jesus."

Elaine's mother miscarried and remained in a coma for two weeks. After a month she finally returned home.

DECLARING OUR TRUE IDENTITIES

Several months later Elaine and her family moved to New Mexico, where they began to rebuild their lives. Elaine's grandmother lived with the family. Elaine's mother reestablished her nursing career while her grandmother took care of the home. She unselfishly cared for Elaine, cooking hot meals every night and reading Bible stories before bed. She attended school functions with Elaine, and on Sundays they walked to church together, where Elaine later met Jack.

For the first time in her life, Elaine felt safe and secure while in the company of a man. Jack was unlike most men she knew from her past. Jack, a premed student with a devout dedication to Christ, treated Elaine with gentleness and love. Jack's compassionate family cooked Sunday dinners for Elaine and her grandmother. They freely shared their love, welcoming them into their Christian home.

After Elaine's high school graduation, her grandmother sewed her wedding dress and helped prepare the young bride for her new future with Jack. While in premarital counseling, the pastor uncovered some of Elaine's past.

Sitting face-to-face with the godly man who was preparing her for marriage, Elaine said, "Pastor, I'm afraid I will become like my father, who was cruel and corrupt."

Fighting tears, she added, "I don't want to be called the 'daughter of evil.' "

The horror in Elaine's eyes and the pain in her trembling voice alarmed the pastor. In a calm voice the pastor said, "Elaine, would you please hand me your Bible?"

She obediently handed him her new Bible. He opened it to the first chapter of John and handed it back to Elaine, asking her to read aloud John 1:12–13. Elaine read, " 'Yet to all who received him, to those who believed in his name, he gave the right to become children of God—children born not of natural descent, nor of human decision or a husband's will, but born of God.' "

Tears slid down Elaine's face as she trembled with relief. "Does that include me?" she asked.

"Yes, Elaine," said the pastor. "The moment you accepted Jesus as your Savior, you became a permanent member of God's family. You are no longer the same person—you are not a 'daughter of evil,' but a daughter of God."

Elaine's pastor marked John 1:12–13 and encouraged her to read it over and over again. "Elaine, every time you have any doubt about who you are today, please open your Bible and read these Scriptures aloud," he said.

This experience changed Elaine's life. She began to see herself as God sees her, not as she viewed herself as a child, and not as others saw her.

"Each time Satan would try to tell me I was doomed for hell because of my biological father," says Elaine, "I would read the marked Scripture aloud.

"Today I know that my real father is Abba, the God who adopted me early in my childhood and who made me a part of his family forever. I can still see the statue of Jesus in my mind—the man in the flowing robes, the one with the outstretched arms. He held me when my life was the blackest, and his peace flowed into me when I most needed it. Indeed, I am born of God."

And so are we. Yes, regardless of what others have said about us, regardless of what images Satan tries to put in our minds, we are daughters of Christ. The instant we accepted Christ as our Savior, we were born of God, and through his authority our identities are changed eternally.

DISCARDING OUR FALSE IDENTITIES

"You were taught, with regard to your former way of life, to put off your old self" (Ephesians 4:22a). In other words, every day we must consciously remind ourselves that our past identities are just that—history.

Today Elaine starts her day by putting on her new nature with a simple prayer. "God, I thank you for removing the pains of my childhood. I acknowledge that I am no longer the 'daughter of evil,' tormented by the violence of my father. Help me to live this day as your daughter, free from the lies of Satan. In Jesus' name, amen."

Now, like throwing old clothes away, Elaine hurls the false identities of her childhood into yesterday's trash. Aware of the Evil One's dark and twisted strategy to destroy her life, Elaine holds on to the truth she savored in John 1:12–13—born of God.

Like Elaine, when we hear "stupid, worthless, shameful, sinful, unworthy, rejected, evil, unwanted," let's remember that these words are garbage and they stink if not disposed of immediately.

UNDERSTANDING OUR NEW IDENTITIES

God is speaking to us—we have new identities. Through faith and belief in Christ we're born of God and have been declared daughters of Christ. We're fully adopted with all the benefits of new identities.

Through God's mercy and grace we can feel free to call him "Abba, Father," which means "Daddy." We can also expect to share in the inheritance of his only son, Jesus. We are heirs of God and joint-heirs with Christ in the Kingdom of God. As believers, our identities are changed forever.

We must understand our new identities because identity precedes and affects behavior, attitudes, emotions, and values. What we do flows from who we perceive ourselves to be.

Someone once said, "Don't try to get in touch with your

feelings; get in touch with truth, and your feelings will change." The truth about who we are and how God sees us can be found in the Bible.

When we first came into this world as babies from our biological mother's womb, we were born of physical bodies into a family. For some, living with our families on earth brought us joy. For others, living with our families brought us pain and anguish, which we must surrender to God. In his infinite wisdom, God designed earthly families to be temporary, giving us the opportunity to become a permanent member of his eternal family.

When we accept Jesus as our Savior, we experience rebirth; simultaneously, we receive the Holy Spirit. When we become Christians, the Holy Spirit comes to live in us, making his temple in our bodies.

A mirror won't reflect the change, but as the Holy Spirit transforms our identities into that of Christ's, we will, over time, see evidence in our lifestyles. We will see patience, gentleness, kindness, love. They become a natural part of our life—our entire spiritual selves will daily become more like Christ. Neil Anderson writes, "As believers, we are not trying to become saints; we are saints who are becoming like Christ."[2]

We become new and vastly improved—we have the Spirit of God living within us. We are now children of God himself. Did you get that? Let's say it again—we are children of God!

What blessings we have inherited. We have been transformed and become someone who didn't exist before. Let's remember that *who we are determines what we do.*

Reaffirming Our New Identities

The following excerpt is from Neil Anderson's book *Who I Am in Christ,* written in first person to inspire each of us as we reaffirm our true identities.

Who I Am in Christ
I Am Accepted in Christ

John 1:12	I am God's child.
John 15:15	I am Christ's friend.
Romans 5:1	I have been justified.
1 Corinthians 6:17	I am united with the Lord, and I am one spirit with him.
1 Corinthians 6:20	I have been bought with a price. I belong to God.
1 Corinthians 12:27	I am a member of Christ's Body.
Ephesians 1:1	I am a saint.
Ephesians 1:5	I have been adopted as God's child.
Ephesians 2:18	I have direct access to God through the Holy Spirit.
Colossians 1:14	I have been redeemed and forgiven of all my sins.
Colossians 2:10	I am complete in Christ.[3]

Christ is speaking to us—let's listen and believe his every word.

In the back of this book, the entire *Who I Am in Christ* (Appendix B) appears as a cutout. Please cut it out. When we read it daily, it helps reaffirm who we are. Read it aloud. These true words from Scripture remind us who we are through Christ. I have taped it to my dashboard. When I really struggle, I tape it to the mirror in my office.

Let's be creative and do whatever it takes to help us believe with all our hearts what God says about us. In time, our behavior will begin to reflect God's image of us.

GROWING IN OUR NEW IDENTITIES

As we grow in God's freedom and power, we will develop a new self-image; the old self-image filled with negative impressions disappears forever. Our self-abusive behaviors—alcohol, drugs, physical abuse, promiscuity, poor health habits, and threats of suicide—fade away as we surrender our old selves to the Lord.

Our growth and change in Christ is a lifelong transition process. Dr. Dan B. Allender states, "Change is always a process. This truth cannot be overemphasized. Many abuse victims feel their progress of change is taking too long. The assumption is that if God is involved, the process will be brief and not too messy. If that were true, then why did God take forty years to teach Moses humility and leadership skills in the sheep fields of Midian? Deep healing, supernatural change, may take years of struggle, trial and error learning, and growing in strength to make the next significant move of faith. No one ought to judge another's growth timetable."[4]

Twenty-three years ago I began my spiritual renewal journey. Like Elaine, there were times I felt like two persons—one who thinks and acts totally opposite to Christ and his righteousness, and the other who watches in disgust and horror.

I think we all struggle with letting go of our old identities and actually living the new. Some days we may go one step forward and two backward; the next day we may gain three steps. As long as we remember who we are in Jesus and keep our focus on the Lord, he will give us the grace to get through the moment, the hour, the day.

Every Christian alive is a work in progress, each with a unique personal growth and change process. This process will continue for all of us until we are standing face-to-face with Jesus himself.

—————————————— PRAYER ——————————————

Father God, how do I begin to thank you? How do I show you my humble appreciation for taking me, a downcast and rejected woman, into your kingdom as your daughter? Lord, I bow down to you and surrender my past identities. Father, I no longer claim to be the person of my past, but I press on, claiming my victorious identity as survivor, overcomer, and daughter of Christ.

Father, teach me your ways so I can live my new identity in a manner that is pleasing to you. Teach me to be the princess that glorifies you in all that I do.

Thank you, Father, for never giving up on me and for loving me through all the changes laid before me. Teach me total surrender so I can embrace your unconditional love with a new and thankful heart. In Jesus' name, AMEN.

CHAPTER EIGHT
Embracing God's Love

*Love the Lord your God with all your heart and with all
your soul and with all your mind.*
MATTHEW 22:37

🌼

"Although I made A's and Bs throughout school, I felt stupid
and incompetent. At fifteen I remember running to wish my
mother well as she left for the hospital to deliver her last baby.
I tripped over a chair. Mama glared at me and yelled, 'Look
out, stupid!' I wondered why Mama didn't seem to love me.
For some reason she always remained aloof. When my young-
est brother came along, she showered him with love. It made
me feel something was wrong with me. After years of trying to
win Mama's love, I finally gave up," says Gayle.

For many of us, before we accepted Christ as our Savior,
embracing any kind of love brought only hurt and rejection.
Like Gayle, we often gave up because of past rejection and
maltreatment. We created a shield to protect our hearts from
pain, establishing our own rules to keep love and anticipated
hurts at a distance.

Now that we know Jesus as our Savior, we don't *need* to
win his love. In the last chapter, we claimed our identities as
daughters of Christ with permanent membership in God's family. In this family, we will learn that we can love freely without
fear of rejection, violation, or pain. Jesus doesn't lie; he will
never leave or forsake us. He promises to love us as we've never
been loved—beyond any measure—unconditionally and forever.

OUR LOVE RELATIONSHIP WITH GOD

Whether we realize it or not, God custom-designed us with a yearning for his love from the depths of our hearts.

The psalmist's words in Psalm 42:1–2 describe this longing for God's presence: "As the deer pants for streams of water, so my soul pants for you, O God. My soul thirsts for God, for the living God. When can I go and meet with God?"

The authors of *Experiencing God* ask us, "Would you like to experience life to the full? You may, if you are willing to respond to God's invitation to an intimate love relationship with him."[1]

We can develop an intimate relationship with God through prayer, reading Scripture, praising and worshiping God, developing supportive relationships with other believers, church involvement, and finding time for quiet rest. Throughout the pages of this chapter we'll learn how to do that.

We all thirst for the joy that reaches the deepest parts of us and a love that can't be lost or diminished by our performance or non-performance. This indescribable joy comes only from dwelling in the loving presence of God.

Know that it's okay for us to come as we are. If we wait to embrace God's love until we "get our acts together," we will procrastinate and never fully embrace him. He wants us right now, just the way we are. So what are we waiting for?

EMBRACING GOD IN PRAYER

Within your temple, O God, we meditate on your
unfailing love.
PSALM 48:9

Loving God through prayer is his gift to the strong and the weak, the young and the old, and the saint and the sinner—he excludes no one. God gives us this gift of prayer because he desires intimacy with us.

In his book *The Word Is Very Near You,* Martin Smith says, "What if God does not demand prayer as much as gives prayer? What if God wants prayer in order to satisfy us? What if prayer is a means of God nourishing, restoring, healing, converting us? Suppose prayer is primarily allowing ourselves to be loved, addressed and claimed by God. What if praying means opening ourselves to the gift of God's own self and presence? What if our part in prayer is primarily letting God be giver? Suppose prayer is not a duty but the opportunity to experience healing and transforming love?"[2]

Yes, the sovereign, all-sufficient, all-knowing, and all-powerful God wants us to receive his gift of prayer while he fills us with his love. He wants to speak with each of us. He wants to hear our prayers. Unfortunately, most of us think of prayer as a way to get God's attention; in reality, prayer involves a two-way communication between God and us.

"Fifteen years ago, when I began my walk with the Lord, my prayers were simple ones like, 'Bless me today, Lord,' 'Take care of my family,' 'May I have a good day,'" says Gayle.

"Today I realize that my desire to know and experience God's divine presence is made real through prayer. God hears my praises and responds with love and mercy. God's love prompts me to pray earnestly for others, feeling their pain and agony."

The Bible tells us to pray in the Spirit (Ephesians 6:18), using the Word of God, with all kinds of prayers and requests. When I feel an attack of painful memories coming on, I open my Bible and pray by reading Scripture. For example, I pray, "Keep me safe, O God, for in you I take refuge" (Psalm 16:1). Or, "I have set the LORD always before me. Because he is at my right hand, I will not be shaken" (Psalm 16:8). Praying Scripture allows me to get through the moment while realizing the presence of God.

God delights in giving us the gift of prayer, desiring that

we come near to the One who created us to love. Treasure God's perfect gift of prayer.

EMBRACING GOD BY READING SCRIPTURE

For the word of God is living and active.
HEBREWS 4:12A

God's love is alive and penetrating. We can delight in this love by reading Scripture. God's dynamic word can touch our hearts and change our lives as he converses with us through the very words in our Bibles.

Many times while I ponder God's Word, I receive new understanding of a particular Scripture. Sometimes a Scripture actually leaps from the page and lodges in my heart. In my mind I can hear God saying, *Pay attention, Jan, I'm talking to you.*

Several years after I began journaling about the experiences of my childhood, a friend from Bible study spoke to me about a ministry opportunity.

"Jan, the pregnancy center has a dire need of lay counselors," Nancy said. "Most of the teens come from broken, abusive homes. I suspect with your background, the girls could relate to you. Will you pray about it?"

Of course I would pray about it. But little did I know that God would speak to me through the very words in our Gospel of John Bible study. Later that week while concentrating on my lesson, I reread John 21. In this chapter Jesus challenges Simon Peter, saying, " 'Simon son of John, do you truly love me . . . ?' 'Yes, Lord,' he said, 'you know that I love you.' Jesus said, 'Feed my lambs' " (John 21:15). Jesus then repeats this same conversation, with slight variations, two more times.

I began to realize, through reading this Scripture, that God had picked me, a cracked and broken vessel, to minister to these abused teens. Like Simon Peter, God wanted me to feed his lambs.

When I agreed to help at the pregnancy center, I discovered that so many of the young teens walked in the same shoes I had walked in years ago. From the depths of sexual abuse to pregnancy, I knew their rage and felt their anguish. When I shared my past with these girls, the walls tumbled down, we bonded, and God's love filled our hearts. I was awed.

I fed Jesus' lambs love and compassion through the Word of God while they committed their new lives to him. While serving these girls, Jesus also continued to heal me, remolding me to pour out to others what he pours into me.

We shouldn't be surprised when God stirs us to read our Bibles. What's happening? God is saying, "Come, children, embrace my love."

EMBRACING GOD WITH PRAISE AND WORSHIP
Great is the Lord and most worthy of praise.
PSALM 145:3A

For the Lord takes delight in his people.
PSALM 149:4A

My worship today differs greatly from my worship during childhood. At age seven I recall standing in front of the mirror, facing school picture day with dread. My reflection displayed an ugly, messy, dirty little girl—a "soiled little girl." My hair was tangled, as usual. Rather than risk upsetting my mother by asking for help, I simply took the scissors and cut the tangles out of my own hair. No tangles equaled no family hassles, and no pain. I cut large hunks of tangled masses from my hair, singing, *Jesus loves me, this I know, for the Bible tells me so.* As a child, praising the Lord reassured me of his love.

Now my praise has grown more sophisticated, but it still all stems from that simple statement, "Jesus loves me." I will never cease to praise God for his love for me and for the work he has done in my life. Today as I write this book, I play instrumental praise music in the background for inspiration. Somehow praise music sets me free to describe our divine adventures as overcomers.

When it comes to praise and worship, although we may all have unique preferences, our purpose in worship must be to embrace God's love and bring glory and honor to his name.

Praise and worship allows us to demonstrate our love of the Lord through word, song, or deed. True praise and worship begins in our hearts and acknowledges God as our perfect and only Jehovah, declaring him our all in all. There are no rules or regulations. God created all things for his joy in order to bring glory to his holy name.

The Bible encourages us to praise and worship God in all that we do, reminding us that our praise and worship today is a dress rehearsal for eternity in the Kingdom of God.

Embracing God by Developing Supportive Friendships

*And when two or three of you are together because
of me, you can be sure that I'll be there.*
Matthew 18:20 The Message

Small group Bible studies, Christian retreats, friendships, and families all provide places where we can support one another through Christ and sense God's love for us. We may share various interests with others such as children, hobbies, or sports, but the greatest nucleus of our community with one another is Christ.

Gayle says, "My past created barriers in all of my relationships. I feared if people knew about my past, they wouldn't like me. The shame-filled lies from Satan tainted my ability to trust others or even reach out to them. Then one day I met a woman through church who shared her own abusive past with me. Our faith in God, as well as our similar experiences, created a bond that led to a supportive relationship.

"We shared our stories, timidly at first, but then with genuine honesty. We also shared the pain of living with chronic illness. By faith, we encouraged each other through our darkest moments. We began to learn how to trust each other."

Like Gayle, let us be open and receptive to developing supportive relationships, knowing that we can give and receive God's love through our relationships with others.

EMBRACING GOD IN CHURCH INVOLVEMENT

What better place to come into the Lord's presence and embrace his love for us than church? We gather together to receive strength from God's Word and to publicly bear witness of our faith and trust in God.

After years of not trusting anyone, Gayle slowly warmed to people in the church. She gradually discovered the benefits of being accountable to spiritual leaders, who had been ordained by God to help her. She says, "My fellow church members have now become my extended family, offering their support and unconditional love. During times of crisis or special need, I can always count on my church family to pray for me and provide encouragement. I see God working through these people to love me."

Every church is unique. We can find formal, informal, and casual churches with music ranging from standard hymns to bands with lively praise teams. Some churches offer support groups for adults who endured child abuse, twelve-step programs, small group Bible studies, and counseling.

We all have different needs and preferences. Some of us may enjoy dressing up and singing from a hymnal, while others may prefer casual dress and contemporary music.

Before becoming a member at any church, however, we

must visit several churches and ask questions about doctrine, style of worship, mission statements, and more. Also, we must be sure that the church we choose regards the Bible as the inspired word of God, preaching and teaching the Word in its entirety.

All of us will face different situations throughout our lives that may trigger a setback or an emotional upset. During these times, we desperately need the loving support and prayer of others. Just as an alcoholic needs to remain involved with a support group, we also need to seek a church that can offer prayer and counseling.

Just remember, God is pleased when we attend church; it allows him to embrace us with his love while maturing our faith.

EMBRACING GOD THROUGH QUIET REST

Be still, and know that I am God.
PSALM 46:10A

Our lives are filled with cell phones, e-mail, telephones, television, people, and noisy distractions. We need most of these devices to carry out our jobs; however, sometimes they get in the way of our ability to be still with God.

God doesn't tell us to throw all modern conveniences out the door. He simply asks us to be still so that we might experience his love without distraction. We may find temporary satisfaction by accomplishing certain tasks, but the satisfaction disappears as soon as additional tasks accumulate.

When we eliminate all distractions, putting aside our "things to do" list, we can be still and embrace the warmth of God's love. Once we hear his distinctive voice during this quiet time, we will let all things pass in order to partake of his love-filled presence. Nothing matches his quiet assurance in the depths of our hearts.

No two people will have the same experiences during their stillness, and their approaches are just as varied.

I sometimes just go for a quiet walk where I can be surrounded by nature. I feel especially intimate with the Lord as I touch and feel all things he created for man's enjoyment. Walking along a beach, I am awestruck as I watch the waves wash away my footprints. In my heart it feels like God is washing away my past, with the imprint no longer visible in his eyes. On the beach it's just me and the Lord—no noise, no distraction.

"It took a long while before I learned to rest quietly with Jesus," says Gayle. "In my mind I felt like I needed to be 'doing' for Jesus to earn his love. To make sure my calendar remained full, I'd read the church bulletin and volunteer to help every ministry with need. I prepared meals for the sick, baked cakes for special occasions, served on committees, and visited the elderly. Then the Lord slowed me down. An illness forced me to stop 'doing.' I learned to simply sit and be with Jesus.

"And then one day, I remember waking up with the most radiant and rested feeling. I grabbed a cup of coffee and walked outside to breathe in the fresh morning air. The sunrise that day took on a special hue with the colors more brilliant than I'd ever remembered. I lifted my eyes and looked toward heaven; I knew I was alone with God—I felt his presence. As I gazed at the beauty of the sunrise, I stood motionless like a sponge, soaking up his love. I realize now the value of resting daily in the Lord's love."

Friends, there is no limit to the ways we may embrace God's love through quiet rest. Some find rest through nature, rocking peacefully on a porch swing or sitting on a kitchen chair, meditating. It doesn't matter how or where we find God's loving rest, it just matters that we do it.

EMBRACE GOD'S LOVE TODAY

We now have a safe love relationship built on trust and security. Gone are the days of insecure relationships in which we felt threatened by danger or violation. Our childlike faith, which has never fully trusted before, now marvels at the pure and holy love of God. May we fully grasp the message that God loves us unconditionally, regardless of our pasts. God wants us to embrace his love right now. May we learn to do that.

————————————— PRAYER —————————————

Father God, by your grace I accept the invitation to embrace your unconditional love through prayer, reading Scripture, praise and worship, developing supportive relationships with other believers, church involvement, finding time for quiet rest, and any other way you direct me. I kneel before you, Lord, and pray that out of your glorious riches you may strengthen me with your power through your Spirit in my heart, the controller of my soul. I pray with continuous surrender that I may grasp how wide and long and high and deep is the love of Christ, this love that surpasses knowledge, that I may be filled with the fullness of your presence. Father, as you fill my humble heart with your love, I say to you be the glory. In Jesus' name, AMEN.

Thriving As Transformed Survivors

*I know their pain and will make them good as new. They'll
get a fresh start, as if nothing had ever happened. And
why? Because I am their very own God.*

❀

"Everything seemed different, especially me. I felt an inner
peace I'd never known before," says Debi.

"Day by day, this new-found peace allowed me to experi
ence deeper levels of God's grace, unconditional love, and forgiveness. I felt strangely restored from the inside out.

"Before my aunt died, she told me that I reminded her of
a butterfly—one who struggled from the cocoon but emerged
a new creature with magnificently colored wings."

So it is with us—through Christ, we are brand-new on the
inside. And as we learned in the last chapter, we can embrace
God's love through every aspect of our lives. We're not the
same anymore. Like the butterfly, we're transformed into new
creations.

WHAT IS TRANSFORMATION?

A caterpillar doesn't comprehend its future metamorphosis as
it squirms aimlessly along leafy branches and green plants.
Debi's childhood paralleled the aimless caterpillar. She felt
alone and rejected when she moved to her aunt's home, leaving behind the stepfather who raped her and the mother who

neglected her. She turned to drugs, alcohol, and prostitution in an attempt to mask the pain.

When Debi accepted Jesus as her Lord and Savior, her life began to change.

"I woke up early each morning," says Debi, "hurrying through my breakfast and shower so I could find a quiet place to read my Bible. I couldn't satisfy my new appetite for God's Word. For over a year, I read up to fifty chapters a day. This had to be of the Lord, because I've never been an avid reader. But now I not only read with an insatiable hunger, I even understood and remembered what I read. Some days while I read, the words seemed three-dimensional; I personally related to the stories while God continued to lay my life before me."

Like Debi, the caterpillar has a great appetite and eats constantly, growing to many times its original size. He then spins his cocoon and goes through growth stages, ending in one called a chrysalis. This delicate process changes the creeping caterpillar into a beautiful butterfly with wings of intricate design and vivid colors.

Yes, friends, God is in the transformation business. He alone can transform our guilt, shame, sin, and destructive selfish natures, making us into new creations who radiate freedom from the past. Transformation calls us to surrender and submit to his authority daily and to walk in trust and obedience. Transformation also calls us to humility.

Transformed to Surrender

Several months before Debi met the trucker who shared Jesus' love with her, she felt as though she had nothing to live for. Strung out on drugs and alcohol, she felt overwhelmed by the shame of selling her body daily. She wanted to die.

Debi says, "I had no hope. I knew no one could ever love me. I became desperate and fell into a pit so deep there was no way out. One day I walked toward a downtown overpass and stood there watching the cars traveling toward their destinations. I knew it wouldn't take long. All I had to do was close my eyes and jump. All the memories of my abuse and my mother refusing to believe me, the drugs, and the prostitution tormented me—the stress was too much. I knew if I jumped, *it would all be over in seconds.*

"But standing on the overpass, the love of my children filled my thoughts. I realized that I could never leave them. Trembling with fear and confusion, I walked away. For some reason I just couldn't do it."

The Lord stopped Debi in her tracks and pursued her with a relentless passion. To halt Debi's destruction and lead her on a path of healing, God reminded her of her children.

Debi gave her life to Jesus there in the cab of a truck with a man she didn't know. She literally lifted both palms toward the roof of the truck cab and radically surrendered to Jesus. In desperation, she surrendered her own free will along with her old way of life. By faith, Debi trusted in Jesus for salvation, looking away from her own circumstances to the promises of God.

She finally understood that God didn't see her as a drug user or a prostitute. He saw her as one of his beautiful children whom he loved, who had been broken and bruised by the sins of abuse.

God created us with free will. As free moral believers in Jesus, we have two choices regarding total surrender to him:

1. We can surrender to Jesus and live a life embracing his love while he transforms us, or
2. We can continue to live struggling every moment with our past and present while searching for a non-existent shortcut to temporary freedom.

Think about it. Do we really want to live like a caterpillar the rest of our lives? Not me! I want to be *set free* to spread glorious wings like a butterfly and enjoy the great God-filled adventure before me.

Transformed to Submit

Our very identities, daughters of the King, call us to receive the gift of a new beginning—a Spirit-filled life. As God's daughters, we are now dead to sin and self and alive to God. He now sits on the throne of our new life and pours out his love for us through the Holy Spirit, dwelling in our hearts forever.

As I write these words, I realize that for all of us surrender is not a one-time event. Once we surrender our wills, submission to God's authority becomes a conscious moment-to-moment lifelong decision process.

Every morning when I wake up, I go through the same daily submission process. I pray, "Lord, I agree that I am no longer the soiled little girl from my childhood. I agree I am no longer a slave to my sins or the sins committed against me. I ask that not my will, but your will be done today."

I keep a Scriptural calendar on my desk to remind me: "God's will, not mine." My Bible always stays near me—I even keep one in the car.

All this might sound a bit extreme. If someone had told me all this twenty-five years ago, I would have thought just that; however, experience has painfully taught me that the moment I fail to submit to God's will is the very moment I will say and do things that totally oppose his ways.

Think about it like this: As believers, we're passengers in this great jet piloted by God. Why would we even think about taking the steering wheel away from our sovereign pilot?

Well, from time to time I do try to control the steering wheel of my life. And guess what? I crash. I say hurtful things to other people. I don't use my time wisely. I live for me, not for Jesus. The good news remains that we can stop and regroup by submitting control to God. After all, he did create us and he has a grand eternal plan for each of us.

Five years ago the basis for this book emerged. During this

writing season, I frequently argued with God. "I really don't want to do this, God," I pleaded. "Can't you give me something easy to write?" The temptation to trash this project and forget what God had called me to do entered my mind more than once.

At times, the daily pain of reliving the agony of my past, as well as bearing the indescribable pain of the other survivors in this book, shrouded me. During these moments, the Lord placed an image in the forefront of my mind—me with a crown of thorns on my head, blood dripping on my face, nails in my wrists and ankles. I could hear him whispering, *"Jan, this is not about you. It's not about the survivors. This is about me, your Lord."*

The apostle Paul, who carried the gospel to non-Jews, knew this and said, "I have been crucified with Christ and I no longer live, but Christ lives in me" (Galatians 2:20). Paul's personal encounter with Jesus changed his life.

We, too, can know this experience as we submit to God each moment, allowing our bodies to become Christ's body to use as he wills. Our hearts become his to be filled with his love and compassion. Our minds become free to think his thoughts. Our wills become his to do good for his Kingdom.

TRANSFORMED TO TRUST AND OBEDIENCE

"It seemed as if I could hear Jesus saying, 'Come, follow me.' So I did," says Debi.

Living as a transformed follower of Jesus means that we feel compelled to trust and obey God, not ourselves.

For Debi, this meant a radical change in her lifestyle. As Debi shared in a previous chapter, when she accepted Jesus as her Savior, she supernaturally no longer desired to continue in her lifestyle of prostitution and drugs. Philippians 2:13 explains this change well: "For it is God who works in you to will and to act according to his good purpose."

Debi's new beginning unfolded right before her eyes as she

accepted Christ's invitation to follow him. The Lord led her to a new environment of mature believers who were able to counsel and minister to her through prayer and Scripture. Debi's new God-appointed "family" helped her learn to read the Bible as the inspired Word of God. They made themselves available, sharing her sorrows, grief, and, in time, her joy.

Through her own free will, Debi worked hard to obey the Lord and her new family. After several months, Debi realized her response to obedience became more natural. After transforming her life, God through the Holy Spirit created this desire in Debi to know and obey God's Word.

"Jeanne, a mature woman from church, invited me to join her Bible study on Wednesday evenings," says Debi. "I was hesitant to accept this invitation. Worry consumed me. My mind filled with fear just thinking about these 'church women.' I knew they wouldn't accept me, especially if they learned of my past. In my mind, these women were pure and holy, while my tainted past emitted the stench of sexual abuse, drugs, and prostitution. I realized later that the thoughts and fears in my head stemmed from Satan—he didn't want me to trust and obey Jesus."

Debi's Bible teacher, Jeanne, became her mentor while also assuming the roles of spiritual mother and counselor. Jeanne, a mature believer, wiped Debi's tears and lovingly nurtured her. Like a shepherd, she watched Debi grow and blossom into a devout Christian who could quote Scripture and then apply it to her life.

"Jeanne told me the church scholarship committee voted to provide funds for me to attend a nearby seminary program," says Debi. "She asked me to pray about the seminary opportunities and to communicate my decision within a week.

"I could sense the Holy Spirit leading me as I read Acts 13:2: 'While they were worshiping the Lord and fasting, the Holy Spirit said, "Set apart for me Barnabas and Saul for the work to which I have called them." '

"I prayed, 'Lord, show me.' After I imitated Barnabas and Saul by fasting and prayer, I accepted this opportunity. I felt as if God was preparing and setting me apart for something, though I didn't know what."

Within a few months Debi was adjusted to her new seminary environment.

"After class one day a visiting pastor said, 'Young lady, fear not. God is healing you. He is preparing you to minister to others who have been hurt and abused.' At the time I didn't understand what this man said, and his words didn't have an immediate impact on me.

"One of my class assignments was to write a letter, poem, or a song to God. I sat down before starting the lesson and prayed, asking for the Lord's guidance and direction. I felt a sense of relief as I wrote my song to God.

"The next day the instructor asked me if I would read my assignment. I read the first few words and then began to sing. When I finished singing, the whole class stood up and applauded. Never in my wildest dreams did I think I would write a song to the Lord and sing it in front of a group of people, but God did," says Debi.

Debi's song, "Jesus Laid His Hand On Me," touched me, too, and she graciously agreed to share it in this book:

Jesus Laid His Hand On Me

Verse 1
*I was lost and going nowhere
And my heart filled with despair.
I could see no hope, no future
Then I found a Savior just waiting there.*

Chorus 1
*Then Jesus laid His hand on me,
He changed my heart, blinded eyes now see.
Yes, Jesus laid His hand on me,*

He touched my soul, my life is now set free.

Verse 2
He took a life filled with heartache,
Calmed the raging storms within my soul.
He took upon himself every heartache and
Made my life restored and whole.

Chorus 2
Since Jesus laid His hand on me,
He changed my heart, blinded eyes now see.
Yes, Jesus laid His hand on me,
He touched my soul, my life is now set free.

Verse 3
I am sure at the end of my journey
When I'm crossing Jordan's tide,
I will see my Savior waiting
To welcome me to the other side.

Chorus 3
'Cause Jesus laid His hand on me,
He changed my heart, blinded eyes now see.
Yes, Jesus laid His hand on me,
He touched my soul, my life is now set free.

Words & music by: "Debi"
Copyright 1992

Debi's beautiful song shows how Jehovah-Rapha, Christ the Healer, rescued her during her deepest despair and laid his healing hand on her broken heart. He transformed her inner rage into peace and freedom. As her song says, she is now *set free* and seeks to live a life of trust and obedience to God.

What Jesus did for Debi, he will do for us.

TRANSFORMED TO BE HUMBLE

We in America are definitely not a humble bunch. We see magazines, newspapers, and televisions filled with information on how to build ourselves up, how to increase our self-esteem, and how to be bigger and better than the rest of the world.

This is so contrary to what the Bible tells us. The Bible speaks of humility as a modest estimation of oneself. Humility suggests no pride and arrogance; it is a spirit of deference or submission.

When I think of humility I think of Jesus. He did nothing from selfish ambition or vain conceit, but in humility he always considered the needs of others. Jesus took on the role of a lowly servant with the physical appearance of man, glorifying God in all ways while humbling himself to death on a cross (Philippians 2:3–8).

We can live our lives expecting to be served, or, as trans formed children of God, we can accept our human limitations and rely on the power of the Holy Spirit to create a humble heart in us. We are free to choose our attitude.

A friend from Texas once told me that "if it's truth, it ain't bragging." As a resident of Texas for the past ten years, I can now say this, too, without prejudice. Unfortunately, long before I moved to Texas and long before I rededicated my life to Jesus, pride had become a way of life for me.

I put myself through college and worked my way up the corporate ladder. By the world's standards I was a "success." Proud of my accomplishments, I reminded my peers constantly of what a hard worker they had beside them. I was proud of the big bucks I made, the nice clothes I wore, and the house— all of this from an abused child who had now blossomed.

I didn't like myself much, and I'm sure others around me felt the same way about me. After I trusted Christ as my Savior, I met a remarkable lady at church. I watched her in amaze- ment. I'm sure she didn't realize it, but she had a tremendous impact on my life. She seemed to notice everyone's needs and reached out to help with compassion. She seemed honestly concerned about the welfare of others. The words *I, me, my,* and *mine* did not seem to be part of her vocabulary. I wanted to be like her, and I tried very hard, but I failed miserably.

I finally realized that I could not make myself be humble. I needed to rely on the transforming power of the Holy Spirit. I know firsthand that when we finally let go of ourselves (our concerns, anxieties, self-sufficiency, pride) and let God care for us, then, and only then, will we experience humility.

When God transforms a proud heart into a humble heart, that heart produces a magnificent fragrance of holiness.

LIVING AS TRANSFORMED CREATIONS

The caterpillar must undergo molting and metamorphosis, disintegrating into a blob of liquid without structure or identity, so it can emerge with breathtaking beauty. Everything about this creature has been transformed—its movement, its appearance, and its feeding methods.

And so it is with us—the old self gradually perishes while the new self evolves. We are transformed moment-to-moment, day by day through divine assistance. We are no longer imprisoned by sin, death or our past—we are free to abide in peace, joy, and the perfect will of God. We are *set free*.

God wants each of us to walk in, and fulfill, his perfect will. He delights in our surrender, trust and obedience, and in our God-produced humility.

"Be filled with the Spirit" (Ephesians 5:18b) is God's will for our lives. Our job is to demonstrate:

1. A desire to be filled. As the butterfly yearns for the nectar, we must also be hungry and thirsty for righteousness.
2. Faith in Christ. Just as the caterpillar releases its body for disintegration to be transformed, we are to offer our bodies as living sacrifices to Jesus. Then we will be transformed by the renewing of our minds, living to honor and obey Jesus.
3. Total dependence upon the Spirit. Everything the caterpillar needs for transformation is within him. All we need

for transformation is living within us—the Holy Spirit.

When the transformation is complete, the only similarity between the caterpillar and the butterfly is the DNA. We are the same—though we maintain our unique DNA, everything else is new and improved. The Spirit-filled person in us is a new creation.

—————————— PRAYER ——————————

Father God, I lay my thankful heart before you in appreciation for all that you do and all that you are. I thank you for loving me so much that you make the gift of transformation available to me. Lord, help me to have the faith to give you total control of my life so I might experience the joy and inner peace of living a life of surrender, submission, obedience, faith, trust, and humility. Father, please disintegrate my old self and transform me daily. Yes, Lord, by faith I thirst to be filled with your righteousness, and I surrender full control to the power of the Holy Spirit. Prepare me to be your sanctuary. Help me claim the exciting new life before me so that I may experience you every moment of my life. In Jesus' name, AMEN.

PART FOUR

Pursuing
the Future

CHAPTER TEN

Igniting Our New Hearts

I'll give you a new heart, put a new spirit in you. I'll remove the stone heart from your body and replace it with a heart that's God-willed, not self-willed.
EZEKIEL 36:26 THE MESSAGE

❖

"Instead of leaving my broken heart with God," says Liz, "I snatched it back and tried to fix it myself. When I finally faced the reality of my grandfather's molestation, I fell apart.

"When I was entirely broken and too weak to resist, God invaded every area of my life, changing everything about me. He placed a new heart within me, complete with a burning desire to depend on him."

Total dependence upon the Lord, as we discovered in the last chapter, is part of our ongoing transformation. Everything we need for this transformation process lives within us—the Holy Spirit of God.

The Holy Spirit in us can be compared to a consuming fire that ignites the kingdom life within. Like fire to incense, the Holy Spirit refines and purifies our new hearts until the aroma of his fruit permeates our every pore. As we learn to live by the Spirit, inhaling every breath from his divine power, God proceeds to change us from the inside out while using fire to make the fragrance of our fruit real.

Think of it this way: As fruit appears in an orchard, so the Spirit's power in us produces fragrant attributes such as love, joy, and peace. As we try to cultivate these attributes in our lives, seeking the presence of the Lord, others will inhale the fragrance of Christ within us.

ABIDING IN CHRIST

John 15:5 tells us, "I am the vine; you are the branches. If a man remains in me and I in him, he will bear much fruit; apart from me you can do nothing."

The key word *abide* means to keep in fellowship with Christ so that he can work in and through us to produce his fruits, such as love, joy, and peace. All believers have the Lord's presence in their hearts, but not all believers choose to abide, or remain in the presence of God.

Throughout the Bible we read about people who abided by God and the impact that made in their lives. Moses, for example, entered into God's presence through the cloud pillar on Mount Sinai, where God gave Moses the Ten Commandments. Moses experienced the glory of God and left the place a changed man; his face was radiant.

The magnificent presence of God that changed the world through Moses also lives within us and changes our world. But we must make the daily choice to *abide* with God. Only then will our hearts ignite and produce fruit.

COMPELLING LOVE

But the fruit of the Spirit is love, joy, peace,
patience, kindness, goodness, faithfulness, gentleness
and self-control.
GALATIANS 5:22–23A

When we accept Christ as our Savior, he ignites our hearts and fills them with love, the first and most important fruit. By God's grace and mercy, we receive a new heart so that we may live according to his will, learning to love and be loved. God doesn't give us a new heart because of our own merit or past actions; rather he gives us a new heart because we are now his daughters, and he is our Father and God.

"As an abused child, I lived without a choice to express opposition," says Liz. "Everyone else controlled me—everything in my out-of-control childhood created pain. When my mother refused to believe the truth about my grandfather's sexual aggressions, I held my feelings inside where they abscessed into anger, depression, and low self-esteem.

"These same emotions followed me into my marriage. As an adult I repressed my emotions and tried to control and manipulate my environment and those around me, especially my husband, Doug.

"I wanted our home to be perfect, with every towel folded and stacked neatly in the linen closet. I arranged everything in his closet by color so his attire would coordinate. I insisted on a schedule for everything in our lives from dinner to grocery shopping.

"My demonstration of love to Doug, my faithful, patient, and supportive husband, directly correlated with his submission to my control. Fortunately for Doug, he traveled extensively."

Although Liz became a Christian as a teen and was an active member in her church, she admits that she didn't really know the unconditional love of the Lord. Then one day nearly ten years ago, when God brought to the surface her grandfather's abuse, she crawled to God in desperation, surrendering her broken heart with all its contents.

"Gradually I accepted God's unconditional love in a new and deeper way. I learned to respond to God's love by loving him back without conditions. Over time my love for the Lord and his love for me inundated my entire being. Much to my surprise I found that loving God and letting him love me also freed me to love Doug, and others, without focusing on performance."

Like Liz, God empowers each of us to give and receive

unconditional love through his supernatural unconditional love. The more love we pour out to others, the more love God lavishes upon us. His love for us is a gift—our love for others is a fragrant fruit of his Spirit.

PREVAILING JOY

You have made known to me the path of life; you will fill me with joy in your presence, with eternal pleasures at your right hand.
PSALM 16:11

What is this joy David mentions in this psalm? Obviously David writes about something only God can give him, not merely fleeting happiness linked to circumstances, which can evaporate without notice. David wants the perpetual joy that God provides to all his children who surrender their lives and submit their wills to his authority.

As Liz matured spiritually, she not only learned to love and be loved unconditionally, she also experienced the joy of walking with God and loving his children.

"I led children's ministries in my church with my friend Mary. Over the years we spent many hours together preparing lessons, planning retreats, coordinating revivals, and conducting Bible studies.

"Our trust in each other grew as we shared our life experiences. After prayer one day, Mary said, 'Liz, you probably would be disgusted with me if you knew my past.' "

By this time Liz's healing had come to a pinnacle, so with compassion she listened as Mary, for the first time in her life, poured out the agony of her sexually abusive childhood. Many times during the meeting Mary wanted to abandon the conversation and bolt. For Mary, like many of us, the agony of facing truth debilitated her.

"Initially, I listened to Mary as though paralyzed. I knew I had to divulge my identity of shame-filled victim in order to reach out to her. I prayed silently, asking God to give me freedom to do this while also claiming my identity of healed survivor. As I told Mary my own story, I felt the distinct nudge of the Holy Spirit as a sense of quiet joy filled me with assurance.

"Finally I scooted my chair closer to Mary, cupped her hands in mine, and we prayed. In my mind, God whispered, *'Lift your hands. Help Mary release her heavy burdens.'* We literally lifted our hands heavenward and continued to pray. Mary sobbed, 'Liz, I felt the touch of God. My hands feel like they're floating.'

"I, too, sensed the release and cleansing. For Mary, this emotional response initiated her healing journey. For me, it confirmed my healing while igniting my new heart with joy. I trembled with God's joy as we sang praises in delight of our newness."

Liz experienced the unspeakable joy of abiding in God's love and allowing him to use her.

We, too, can know this eternal true joy of abiding with God. Like Liz, we can emit this fragrant fruit of joy.

Finding Peace

I will lie down and sleep in peace, for you alone, O Lord, make me dwell in safety.
Psalm 4:8

"For years, instead of sleeping at night and resting in peace," says Liz, "my mind filled with nightmares of monsters chasing after me with huge hands. The monsters especially reared their ugly heads while my husband traveled and I slept alone. I often awoke with perspiration-soaked pajamas, consumed with a burning rage, hedged by fear and anxiety. For years I prayed for deep peace and the removal of these nightmares.

"Then one day I got a phone call. I remember the hair on my arms bristled; my stomach convulsed," says Liz. "I listened as the caller described Grandfather's cancer diagnosis. Part of me felt relief that he would soon be out of my life, while the believer in me recognized that his prognosis for eternal hell was far worse than his cancer diagnosis.

"I sobbed hysterically for hours, leaving me trembling from the physical and emotional exhaustion. I glanced in the mirror of the hallway—my image appeared grimy. My heart and mind felt the same way.

"Soaking in the hot bathtub, I tilted my head back and closed my eyes. Over and over in my head I heard God's words: 'Liz, remember, not your will, but mine. The truth will set you free. Pray for those who persecute you—hell is forever.'

"Through prayer, fasting, journaling, and counseling I had released the ugliness of my childhood pain, brought on by my grandfather. I had maintained a sense of peace knowing I didn't own his sins. Now, as God urged me to pray for 'those who persecuted me,' I longed for an even deeper peace.

"Within a couple of days I responded in obedience to the Lord, submitting to his will, not mine," says Liz. "I felt led to call my grandfather. I analyzed my motivation and confirmed that it stemmed from the Lord's love, not mine. I had no pre-conceived notions of any reaction from my grandfather.

"When he answered the phone I held my breath, then exhaled. 'Do you remember all those times you made me sit with you and I didn't want to? I want you to know that everything you did to me was inexcusable.'"

Liz's grandfather, now frail from the cancer, offered no explanation, except he said over and over between sobs, "I'm sorry. I'm so sorry, Liz."

"The only reason I can accept your apology is because of the forgiveness God has given me," Liz said. "If it had been up to me, it wouldn't have been possible."

Liz then told her grandfather about God's love and

explained to him the way of salvation through Jesus. She said good-bye. As she hung up the phone, she experienced her heart filling with a deep peace she had never encountered in her life. When she lay down to sleep that night, she slept as she never had before, with no monsters attacking her.

By submitting to the power of God, Liz felt motivated to confront her grandfather with truth while also sharing God's plan of salvation with him. As believers, God equips us to share the love of Jesus with sinners regardless of their life circumstances. Remember, this is not about us and it's not about the sinner; it's about allowing the power of God to live in us and control us.

Before attempting confrontation as Liz did, we must seek the guidance of wise counsel and examine our motives. Confrontations are unpredictable, at best. Based on my lay counseling and personal experience, most abusers deny truth and become defensive.

Confronting our abusers is a personal matter with no rigid guidelines to follow. Some of us can accomplish safe and truthful confrontation by writing a letter and not mailing it, journaling, writing a poem, drawing a picture, or writing a story for publication. We must remember that confrontation is for *our* healing, so we need to do what is in *our* best interests. The Holy Spirit prompts us while directing us to follow him on the road to peace.

Just as Jesus calmed the waters during the storm on the Sea of Galilee, he will create calm and peace within us. He is our refuge and our fortress during every storm. He may not remove every trial or difficult circumstance from our lives, but he will always provide the calm and strength to weather the storm.

An initial internal sense of peace begins when we accept Christ as our Savior. It grows deeper in our *new* hearts as we remain faithful to God regardless of circumstances. The Lord's peace can fill us with the confidence to face the present and the future without fear. His peace will guard our hearts and minds and deliver us from evil. This unique peace is God's gift to us.

ILLUMINATING THE FLAME

[Jesus] will ignite the kingdom life within you, a
fire within you, the Holy Spirit within you,
changing you from the inside out.
MATTHEW 3:11B THE MESSAGE

Our new hearts are ablaze by the power of God's divine nature within us. He chose us, the improbable, to receive these new hearts and bear fruit that glorifies him. How encouraging for us to know that our new hearts are capable of producing the fruit of love, joy, peace, patience, kindness, goodness, faithfulness, gentleness, and self-control. What's more, others will see and experience Christ in us through our fruit.

When Liz's husband saw the changes in her ability to love him without conditions, he also experienced the power of God. Even though Doug believed in God, by experiencing Liz's unconditional love for him, he also came to know the love of Jesus.

Think about it: God allowed Mary and Liz to serve together within their church as leaders of the children's ministry, where their trust and friendship divinely flourished. When Mary's heart began to crumble from the abuses of her childhood, God used Liz to attest to his healing power. He poured hope into Mary while anointing Liz with the fragrance of true joy.

Liz, once a timid woman filled with fear and anxiety, now knows the deep peace that withstands the turbulence of the world. Her peace does not depend on circumstances, past experiences, or future promises; it rests in the security of her salvation through Jesus. Today Liz has been married nearly twenty-five years. Her new heart illuminates the flame of

Christ daily, gracing others with the fruit of the Spirit.

What God did for Liz he'll do for us. Our new hearts are free, and the flame of the Holy Spirit of Jesus stands ready to keep us ignited with a fire that can't be extinguished.

──────────────── PRAYER ────────────────

Father God, I thank you for removing my heart of stone and replacing it with a new supple heart filled with the Holy Spirit. Lord, I thank you for giving me the capacity to love you and others. Through you, Lord, I am safe and secure. The privilege of the Holy Spirit abiding in me, and I in him, is such a beautiful gift, and I thank you. Father, you have shown me by surrendering myself to you and accepting the suffering that I can soar to new heights, radiating your beauty while igniting my new heart. Yes, Lord, I welcome your presence so that I may be a bearer of your fruit of the Spirit. Thank you for loving me so much that you consider me worthy of your fruit. In Jesus' name, AMEN.

CHAPTER ELEVEN

Living in Freedom: Improbable Overcomers

Being confident of this, that he who began a good work
in you will carry it on to completion until the day of
Christ Jesus.
PHILIPPIANS 1:6

✿

"I'm free from my former drug and alcohol addictions," Debi says. "I'm no longer a nine-year-old child raped by a relative and made to feel like filth. The bitterness and rage of my past has disappeared. My old self is gone—today I'm a daughter of Christ, filled with an inexpressible joy."

Like Debi, our joy doesn't come from our circumstances or feelings—it springs from a thankful attitude for what Christ does in and through us. When someone asks about our pasts, God says, "What past? She has no past. When she came to me, I forgave her, she forgave herself, and she has learned to forgive others."

GOD'S RAINBOW

When God flooded the earth and destroyed everything except Noah and those protected in the ark, he provided the covenant of the rainbow and promised never to destroy the world again by floods. By setting that rainbow in the sky, God demonstrated his faithfulness to his work of grace. God chose not to act in his power to destroy, but instead to walk beside, carry, and restore us. The rainbow signifies God's gift of hope—unconditional and eternal—bearing witness to his love for mankind. We see God's rainbow in our lives when—after the thunder blasts, lightning bolts through the sky, and rain pounds the ground—the storm finally breaks.

In chapter one, we met broken victims of yesterday. We experienced their pain as they tried to live without God. We watched as God redeemed their broken hearts and placed them next to his. We saw God breathe new life into them, releasing them from their pain and anguish, and allowing them to be *set free* from their pasts.

Throughout the subsequent chapters, we weathered the storms with these brave overcomers, feeling the agony of their rage, rejection, and pain. As they surrendered their lives, we, too, embraced God.

Under God's rainbow, as we read in the last chapter, he continuously renews and transforms our hearts—*setting us free* to be victorious overcomers. Friends, let us rejoice with our fellow overcomers as we now look at their lives today.

❀

THE FORMER DAUGHTER OF EVIL
Elaine's Story

"I don't watch *Leave It to Beaver* anymore," says Elaine. "I don't need to—I have a better family. I'm no longer the daughter of a gangster; I'm a daughter of Christ.

"As a child growing up, I often wondered *why me*? Why did my childhood have to be filled with violence? Why did I have to fear for my life at the hands of my own father? Why didn't I have loving parents?

"For years I didn't talk about my past with others. I feared if I talked about my father's criminal activity, the circumstances of his death, the violence I endured as a child, then it meant I hadn't changed. And I feared people would reject me.

"Initially I shared my story with a select few who were experiencing similar pain. Then my pastor asked me to be a volunteer lay counselor and Bible study shepherd within our church to a new group of older teen girls and young adult women. The old me wanted to say no, and run. But I agreed to sit in and observe a few sessions before making a commitment.

"The casual setting created a non-threatening, comfortable environment. We all wore jeans and sat on the floor with our Bibles and notebooks. The younger women checked me out, from the shoes on my feet to the creases in my face. *They don't trust me*, I thought. *Maybe I'm not supposed to be here.*

"After the meeting had begun, I noticed a young man enter the room and tap the lady to my left on the shoulder. I watched as she cried, gathered her things, and stood up to leave the room.

"Being a reserved person, I tried to ignore the feelings that stirred in me. But I found myself following this woman out of the room, asking her if I could help. I froze when Anna replied, 'I have to leave. My dad broke a beer bottle over my mother's nose.' *Oh, the numerous times I left events because my dad had injured my mom. Yes, Lord, I think you placed me here for these girls.*

"'You don't know what it's like to live like me,' Anna sobbed.

"'Yes, Anna, I do know what it's like,' I said.

"These women live the life I lived, experiencing physical and emotional abuse while others daily violate their safety and security. They eagerly listen now while I tell them how my hope in Jesus transformed me, a perceived daughter of evil, in spite of my tragic childhood. I now counsel others one-on-one, as well as in group settings, while helping them overcome healing hurdles.

"Why me? I'm humbled to think the Lord can use me to serve him and help others. I believe the Lord has given my life a new purpose by allowing me to be a part of this ministry, sharing his hope with those who walk the same steps I walked over thirty years ago.

"I'm still married to the man I married more than twenty-five years ago; his faith and spiritual maturity continue to inspire me. We have a grown son and a daughter-in-law. Now that I am healed, I feel called to do for others what the Lord has done for me. To this I say, 'Yes, Lord!'"

❊

THE FORMER KEEPER OF SHAMEFUL SECRETS
Liz's Story

"Until I faced the truth about my grandfather and the sexual abuse," says Liz, "my attitude reflected one of denial and a cold indifference toward others. When I heard others speak of various childhood pains and trauma, I thought to myself, *Get over it already. It's in the past, you can't do anything about it, so just move on.* I felt if I could move on, so could they. In reality, I hadn't faced the truth about my internal damage from the sexual abuse. Then I hit bottom and reluctantly admitted the truth. That was when I found hope.

"I developed a close relationship with our church's director of women's ministry, and she became my mentor. She ministered to many women with mercy and love. Some time ago she asked me to share my testimony at a women's retreat. I felt hesitant and fearful at first, but she assured me that she had prayerfully considered the request before coming to me. This retreat served as the launching pad for Christ to use me to reach other women.

"Now every time the Lord presents opportunities to share my testimony before other women, he blesses me, and through him they experience blessing. Women come up to me after my testimony and share their stories of childhood abuse with me.

"An elderly lady with a caustic attitude approached me at a grocery store some time after hearing my testimony. She said, 'I've experienced disaster after disaster throughout my life. Tell me, Liz, how can you be so joyful after such a terrible child-hood?'

"Delighted with her question, I replied, 'Oh, I'm not that same little girl. Somehow I've gotten through the pain. Thanks to Jesus, my identity is not child of abuse, it is child of God.' We met again during a group luncheon weeks later and I noticed a new tenderness about her. *Perhaps she has begun to release her pain.*

"It seems the more I share my testimony and reach out to other women with wounded pasts, the more I grow and mature spiritually. Even in responding to Jan's questions for this book, God ministered to me and brought healing in ways I hadn't thought possible. In addition, the opportunity to ver-balize in writing the healing process has broadened my scope of God's grace. Someday I want to write words of encourage-ment and hope for Christian publications.

"God's healing in my life has changed my relationships with my husband, children, and other family members. I'm a better wife and mother because I am not bogged down with the identity of a shame-filled victim. I'll always be a sinner in need of the Lord's grace; however, my new identity in Christ frees me to be the person God designed me to be."

✿

THE FORMER PROSTITUTE
Debi's Story

"I thank God for stopping my foolish attempt at suicide on the overpass by reminding me of my children," says Debi. "When I later hitchhiked across the States, God placed a truck driver in my life who shared the Gospel with me and led me to accept Christ as my Savior. For that I am forever grateful.

"I'm thankful for the kind people, my heroes, who self-lessly helped me leave a destructive life of drugs, alcohol, and prostitution. Jeanne, my first guidance counselor, always made time to meet with me when I spiraled downward.

"I can still hear the tenderness in Jeanne's voice as she held me in her arms and whispered, 'Debi, I can feel your tears against my cheek. I promise we'll get you through this day without one sip of beer. Did you know your tears dispense a pleasing fragrance to Jesus?' Her words made an indelible mark upon me. How I cherish the loving kindness of the individuals who helped me get by, one day at a time.

"I now realize that when I visited my first women's Bible study, the Lord began preparing me to love and trust other women. Initially I felt threatened by the 'church ladies' surrounding me. I feared if I told them the truth about my past, they would judge and reject me. Much to my surprise, they encouraged and supported me without judgment.

"Someone once told me that the problems I've faced would be the catalyst to help others, and I always thought to myself, *yeah, right.* But over the years, women both young and old have indeed allowed me the privilege of walking alongside them, wiping their tears, and encouraging them through my past.

"Probably one of my greatest blessings is watching the hopeless regain hope through Jesus. I'm able to observe the day-to-day growth of women close to me. Most of the women who work with me call me Mom, and in God's eyes, I *am* their spiritual mother.

"If you had told me twenty years ago that I'd be an ordained pastor, counseling broken women, I probably would have laughed and walked away in disbelief. Not in my wildest dreams did I imagine God would use a rebellious outcast like me in his Kingdom, but he does.

"I'm not perfect. I continue to make mistakes, but I feel reassured when friends and family who have seen the gradual, steady changes in my life realize that only God could perform such a drastic transformation. My daughter, Laurie, watched my transformation and then felt compelled to commit her own life to the Lord. Today we work together serving women the Lord brings into our lives.

"People don't care how much I know about the Bible," says Debi, "or how well I teach. They first want to know that I care for them and love them right where they are. I may slip and fall, but the changes the Lord has made in me are permanent. God gets the glory, and I say, 'Thank you.'"

❀

THE FORMER ATTITUDE OF DEFEAT
Gayle's Story

"Mama's constant degrading words caused me to have a low self-image with a persistent sense of defeat," says Gayle. "To cope with the doubt and rejection, I detached from people and kept a safe emotional distance. I see now how Satan used this bondage to isolate me from God and others.

"I've now found victory over darkness with God in control. I'm no longer a slave to the sins of rejection and defeat. I'm a new creation. The old me has vanished, and the new me remains forever thankful to Jesus. I no longer avoid relationships, because God is removing the fear that held me back. Through the Holy Spirit's leading, I can now visibly see the pain and anguish in others. I feel moved to action when someone loses a family member or becomes hospitalized.

"God directed me to two prayer ministries for the chronically ill. With my gifts of mercy and compassion, I find I can love and encourage people on almost a daily basis.

"Robert, a good friend who lived with the agony of cancer for several years, loved all of nature, but he particularly admired the eagle, which he had emblazoned on his truck. Throughout his home he had eagle oil paintings and porcelain figurines. To encourage him, I once sent him a note with some words from the book of Isaiah. Before his death, he wrote me a note saying, 'Gayle, the Isaiah 40:31 Scripture with the eagle in the faded background renewed my hope and strength. Probably in heaven I will soar on the wings of eagles and not grow weary. Today I'm grateful for your prayers and encouragement.'

"How amazing that the Lord allows me to comfort people dying of cancer, grieving relatives and friends, childhood abuse survivors, and others who need prayer and support. The old me would have shied away from involvement, but the me who is a healed overcomer says, 'I can do it through Christ.'"

❖

THE FORMER PARTY GIRL
Karissa's Story

"I stand in wonder as I remember the evening before my accident when I prayed for the Lord to change me. As I slept that night, I had no idea of the changes ahead of me that would rearrange and transform my entire life from the inside out.

"God not only saved my life after the truck ran over me, but he also gave me a new one. Everything about me is new—from the pig's mitral valve in my heart to the new spiritual heart from God.

"I will never forget the day I met my neighbor Sam in the hallway of my apartment complex, where he nearly ran me over with his electric wheelchair. Sam, a victim of multiple sclerosis, lived alone. Over the next few months our relationship grew from neighbors to friends. I eventually mustered up the courage to ask him about his faith.

"'I got saved a long time ago,' he said. His face reddened and the intensity of his voice strengthened. 'Do I believe in Jesus? Sure, Karissa. I believe I'm mad at him.'

"After Sam moved to a full-care facility, I arrived one day with Sam's favorite meal—hamburger, fries, and a Coke. He looked disheartened and tired, like a worn-out rag doll.

"Feeding him humbled me. Over eleven years earlier, someone had fed me as I sat in a wheelchair. Only in my case,

I knew the impermanence of my situation. My heart ached for Sam. As if reading the sympathy on my face, he yelled, 'I hate this place. I hate my life. I hate . . .'

"I cringed as Sam spat out anger toward life and toward God. *Lord, help me reach out to him.* 'Sam,' I said, 'being a Christian doesn't guarantee that we'll never suffer. But I have learned that no matter how I feel, God promises good for my life. I choose to believe him and not allow bitterness to control me. You can do the same.'

"Sam now rides his electric wheelchair to a church one block from the nursing home. He anticipates meeting Jesus in heaven and has decided his life doesn't belong to him, but to Jesus. Sam even shares the Gospel with his roommate and the residents of the nursing home.

"It's ironic that my past sufferings bring encouragement and hope to others. The Lord has placed me in crisis-hotline ministries for troubled teens, hospital visitation, and prayer ministries, feeding the homeless with spiritual and edible food, and attending to the spiritually sick. I share my testimony with groups and churches and write stories about my experiences, five of which have been published in different inspirational anthology books.

"I don't know what God has planned for me tomorrow, and it doesn't matter because *I now know that my physical heart may fail, but my spiritual heart lives forever.*"

❧

THE FORMER HARDENED HEART
Gloria's Story

"The years of sexual, emotional, and physical abuse nearly destroyed me," says Gloria. "It took years for my heart to harden, and it has taken more years to remove all the rocks and hard clods from my heart; in fact, it's still a day-to-day process.

"Eventually God replaced my anger with empathy for my

mother, who suffered more than fifty years from the darkness of mental illness. When God healed me, I could finally comprehend that the drugs and treatment administered to my mother never adequately treated her illness. Had she suffered today, modern drugs and therapy, combined with God's healing, could have provided a higher quality of life for her—and for me.

"During Mom's last few years, she received Christ as her Savior through a national Christian organization. God, in his sovereignty, filled her with a peace that most people couldn't understand. I know for certain she's in heaven, and I thank the Lord for the miraculous wonders in my mother's last years. Although still plagued with mental illness, she died at peace with me, the Lord, and herself.

"God's healing process in my life has not been an occasional experience; it's an all-consuming process that requires my complete cooperation. I've recognized that submitting to the Lord begins with acknowledging that God loves me unconditionally and forever. That gives me the courage to stay on the straight and narrow path of healing with a thankful heart.

"Through it all, I survived. I'm no longer the dirty little girl who went to school smelling awful—she's history. My attitude of bitterness and anger toward my abusers has perished, as well.

"For a long time I prayed for God to use me, but I knew I had a long way to go. Years later I'm finally usable in God's kingdom here on earth.

"Through Christ I'm able to reach out to other victims of child abuse who need words of encouragement, a hand to hold, and wisdom to share that only comes from someone who has walked before them and received God's gift of healing. The Lord has called me to share my healing testimony with women in urban ministries, unconventional schools for delinquent teens, shelters, recovery houses, and more. An alarming percentage of these women, as high as 95 percent, have experienced abusive childhoods.[1] God uses my testimony to offer his hope to these lost and broken victims.

"I remain forever grateful for God's lifelong healing process."

THANKFUL RESPONSE

The essence of our new hearts is our thankful response to God's call on our lives. As we walk through life, let us demonstrate our thankfulness to the Lord by influencing others in our actions, deeds, and words through the loving presence of the Holy Spirit within us. As others see the changes in us, we plant the seeds of Christ's Kingdom in them.

Every day we will experience both victory and defeat, but through Christ we will learn and grow from every single experience. Every day we will encounter new situations, trials, and temptations. Our healing journey will not be complete until we stand face-to-face with Jesus.

I can't say with 100 percent certainty that I am thankful for all my past painful experiences; however, I can say with 200 percent confidence that I stand continually amazed that the Lord finds good use for all the suffering and grief I've endured. As a speaker and author, I stand in awe as God uses my humble brokenness to touch the hearts of audiences from all walks of life while remolding my character and transforming me with his power and might. Be prepared; your testimony will one day help others.

Which story is mine? Which story is yours? From the shame-filled little girl who endured physical, sexual, and emotional childhood abuse through the horrid years of a life bent on self-destruction, probably a piece of both of us can be found in each story.

The good news is that God does not waste one single ounce of our pain.

Like "The Chosen Vessel" in chapter one, I have poured

out to you the love, compassion, and healing that the Lord has poured into me. As the author of this book and a vessel to share God's love, I thank you for the privilege of sharing the power of God's love and grace.

Until we meet face-to-face, I give you the prayer below from my heart to yours.

──────────────── PRAYER ────────────────

Father God, I thank you for the privilege of holding the hands and hearts of each precious reader throughout this healing journey. Lord, I ask that you keep their new hearts next to yours, breathing new life into them every moment of the day to sustain them. God, you are so gracious to allow me to walk with you as you heal and work wonders in the lives of my new friends and sisters in Christ. I thank you, Lord, and praise you for all that you've done and all that you're going to do in them. Through your grace, Lord, I know they will be set free. In Jesus' name, AMEN.

DISCUSSION QUESTIONS

These discussion questions are designed for both individual and group participation. They will help you discover for yourself how to use Scripture and the journeys of others to guide you during your healing journey.

If you are using *Set Free* in a group atmosphere, you will need to appoint a facilitator to lead the group's participants in discussion and encourage all participants to verbalize their answers and discoveries. Use Scripture to keep the group focused on God rather than members' opinions or attitudes.

CHAPTER ONE

1. Jesus said, "You did not choose me, but I chose you" (John 15:16). How does it make you feel to be chosen by Jesus?

2. The beginning of chapter one quotes portions of a poem titled "The Chosen Vessel." The poem describes how God passed by the gold, silver, and brass urns and chose the clay vessel. Think about the reasoning behind this choice. Why did God choose the clay vessel?

3. In what ways do the improbable women in this chapter resemble the clay vessel?

4. When Elaine got off the church bus, Pastor John said, "Remember, Elaine, Jesus loves you." Based on Elaine's home environment, how could Pastor John's words impact Elaine's life?

5. "It doesn't matter who we were yesterday or what we did— what matters is that God wants to do something with our

lives today." What is this statement saying to you personally?

6. Why does God desire to transform and heal improbable women?

CHAPTER TWO

1. In John 8:44, Jesus calls the devil "the father of lies." Reflect for a moment on Gloria's story. How did the lies of the devil influence Gloria's childhood?
2. In what ways do you identify with Gloria's pain?
3. What is your key defense against the evil principalities of the world?
4. As God's only son, what sort of abuse did Jesus suffer?
5. Why did Jesus die?
6. Jesus chose you—to love you as you've never been loved before. What else does Jesus desire to do in your life?
7. What steps can you take to have a personal and loving relationship with Jesus?

CHAPTER THREE

1. In the eyes of others, Karissa was a drug-using party girl. How did God see her?
2. Who is God?
3. What does God look like in your life?
4. Where was God during Karissa's accident?
5. What good came from Karissa's accident?
6. In Exodus 15:26, God says he is the "Lord who heals you." Why does God heal?

CHAPTER FOUR

1. Psalm 62:8 says, "Trust in him at all times . . . pour out your hearts to him." What circumstances in your life has God orchestrated to help you face the truth about your past? How can you begin your truth-building journey with the Lord?

2. For years, Gayle evaded the truth about her childhood. To escape her parents, she chose to marry a boy from high school. In what ways can you relate to Gayle's past victim survival mode?
3. Admitting truth with, "Yes, I was abused, and the abuser stole something from me that I will never get back," is an important step to pouring out your heart. What truths in your life are you beginning to admit to yourself?
4. Gayle's counselor encouraged her to journal her experiences and feelings. Journaling helps you sort out abusive memories while providing the freedom to speak truth. To help you journal, try writing a few thoughts while filling in the blanks below.

God, I write you to express a few truths about my past. The pain that hurts the most is hard to write about, but I'll do my best:

_____

_____

_____

_____

_____

_____

_____

_____

Prayer:
    Father, remind me that admitting truth doesn't mean I'm resigning myself to it; it means truthfully admitting my pain so I can move on and be *set free*. In Jesus' name, amen.

CHAPTER FIVE

1. If God took a spiritual stethoscope to your heart today, what would he see?
2. Karissa felt imprisoned by the lies of Satan, her past sins, as well as the sins committed against her. How did these lies and sins impact Karissa's life?
3. How have the consequences of lies and sins impacted your life?
4. Regardless of your past or present, how does the Lord feel about you?
5. First John 1:9 says, "If we confess our sins, he is faithful and just and will forgive us our sins and purify us from all unrighteousness." What methods is God using in your journey to make known your unconfessed sin?
6. According to Psalm 51:17 (THE MESSAGE), "Heart-shattered lives ready for love don't for a moment escape God's notice." How does this Scripture apply to you?

CHAPTER SIX

1. Psalm 55:22 says, "Cast your cares on the LORD and he will sustain you." What are these burdens and how can they affect your life?
2. How does the truth of Philippians 4:13, "I can do everything through him who gives me strength," relate to the release process?
3. How did Debi finally gain freedom from her abusers?
4. In what ways can you relate to Debi's initial resistance to release her abusers?
5. What happened when Jan said, "Lord, I'm not capable of this type of forgiveness"?
6. Why does the Lord want every part of you to be *free*?

CHAPTER SEVEN

1. When you receive Jesus as your Savior, you are given a new identity. How do you feel about this privilege?

2. In what ways can you relate to Elaine feeling like two persons?

3. Elaine's pastor instructed her to read John 1:12–13: "Yet to all who received him, to those who believed in his name, he gave the right to become children of God—children born not of natural descent, nor of human decision or a husband's will, but born of God." How can this Scripture help you during times of fear and doubt?

4. How does the truth found in the excerpt from Neil Anderson's *Who I Am in Christ* make you feel?

5. Pause for a few moments and reflect on your new identity, then ask yourself, "Who am I?"

6. In order to be transformed, what should you do with your past identities?

7. When will your unique personal growth and change process be complete?

CHAPTER EIGHT

1. Matthew 22:37 says, "Love the Lord your God with all your heart." Why did Gayle find it hard to embrace God's love?

2. In what ways can you relate to Gayle's childhood experiences?

3. What does it mean to embrace Jesus just the way you are?

4. How does prayer work in your efforts to embrace the love of Jesus?

5. How could your life change if you set aside regular quiet time to embrace Jesus' love?

6. What friendship and support groups do you participate in to feel the love of Jesus and fellow believers?

7. When you embrace God's love, how do you feel inside?

CHAPTER NINE

1. Zechariah 10:6 (THE MESSAGE) says, "I know their pain and will make them good as new." How does God do this?

2. Debi's life paralleled the metamorphosis of the butterfly. What similarities to the butterfly do you see in your transformation?

3. By faith Debi gave up and surrendered to Jesus. She found new freedoms. What freedoms can you find in your surrender journey?

4. Debi said, "It was as if I could hear Jesus saying, 'Come, follow me.'" What did following Jesus require in Debi's life? What does following Jesus require in your life?

5. Reading Debi's song, *Jesus Laid His Hand On Me,* what feelings were aroused in you?

6. When you become a new creation, what are you *set free* from?

7. When you receive your new beginning, what happens?

CHAPTER TEN

1. Ezekiel 36:26 says, "I will give you a new heart and put a new spirit in you." Why does God give you a new heart?

2. How is your new heart ignited?

3. What happened to Moses on Mount Sinai?

4. How did Liz's childhood impact her marriage?

5. John 15:5 tells us, "I am the vine; you are the branches. If a man remains in me and I in him, he will bear much fruit; apart from me you can do nothing." How can you bear much fruit? What kind of fruit is Jesus referring to in this Scripture?

CHAPTER ELEVEN

1. Where do your joy and thankfulness spring from?

2. The rainbow is God's gift of hope—unconditional and eternal—signifying his love for you. During your healing journey to be *set free*, what rainbows have you seen in your life through prayer, praise and worship, Scripture, quiet rest, fellowship, and support groups?

3. How did you feel when you saw Elaine's life playing out before her through Anna?

4. Liz's life was once filled with shameful secrets. What is her life like today?

5. How have the problems in Debi's life become a catalyst to help others?

6. Romans 6:18 says, "You have been set free from sin and have become slaves to righteousness." How has the Lord set Gayle free from her sins of doubt and rejection?

7. As Karissa tried to reach out to Sam, she said, "I've learned that no matter how I feel, God promises good for my life." How can Karissa's words to Sam help you during your healing journey?

8. How does Gloria describe God's healing process?

9. As you reflect on the victories of the improbable women, what have they been *set free* from?

10. Through God's grace, what have you been *set free* from?

Names of God

Psalm 76:1 tells us God's name is great. His name reveals his relationship to us while also identifying his very nature and character. In Scripture, the names of God convey his promises, relationships, authority, and power.

There was and is one true and living God—One God in three persons: God the Father, God the Son, and God the Holy Spirit—the Trinity. The Bible speaks of all three members—the Trinity—united as one. God is a non-material, self-existent spiritual being.

The names of God are helpful in understanding scriptural passages: When the Bible speaks of Jehovah, it refers to the Godhead—God the Father, God the Son, and God the Holy Spirit.

As you thank God for who he is and what he is doing in your life, praise and honor him by acknowledging his names. I encourage you to add "my" in front of his name, where appropriate, to help you create a deeper level of intimacy.

God the Father
Abba (Daddy)
Almighty
Creator
Father of Compassion
Faithful God Who Does No Wrong
Forgiving God

God my Maker
God my Rock
God of Comfort
Great, Mighty, and Awesome God
Hiding Place
Hope
Light
Maker of Heaven and Earth
Master in Heaven
Mighty Rock
Refuge
Refuge in the Day of Disaster
Refuge in Times of Trouble
Rock of Our Salvation
Shelter from the Storm
Shepherd
Source of Strength
Strong Deliverer
Support

Jesus—God the Son
Alpha and Omega
Author of Life
Christ Jesus My Lord
Christ Jesus Our Hope
Christ of God
Eternal Life
Faithful and True Witness
Friend
God Over All
Holy and Righteous One
Immanuel (God With Us)
Intercessor
Jesus Christ our Lord

Jesus Christ our Savior
King of Kings
King of the Ages
Lamb of God
Light of the World
Living Bread That Came Down From Heaven
Lord and Savior Jesus Christ
Messiah
Prince of Princes
Rock Eternal (Rock of Ages)
Ruler of God's Creation
Savior of the World
Shepherd
Son of the Most High God
Wonderful Counselor
Word of Life

God the Holy Spirit
Breath of the Almighty
Holy Spirit of God
Spirit of Counsel and of Power
Spirit of Faith
Spirit of Fire
Spirit of Glory
Spirit of God
Spirit of Grace and Supplication
Spirit of Holiness
Spirit of Jesus Christ
Spirit of Judgment
Spirit of Justice
Spirit of Knowledge and of the Fear of the Lord
Spirit of Life
Spirit of Our God
Spirit of Sonship (adoption)
Spirit of the Living God

Spirit of the Lord
Spirit of the Sovereign Lord
Spirit of Truth
Spirit of Wisdom and of Understanding
Spirit of Wisdom and Revelation
Voice of the Almighty
Voice of the Lord

The illustrative names listed were gleaned from *Experiencing God*[1] and are illustrative, not comprehensive.

Who I Am In Christ* and
What Matters

Who I Am in Christ

I am accepted . . .

John 1:12	I am God's child.
John 15:15	As a disciple, I am a friend of Jesus Christ.
Romans 5:1	I have been justified.
1 Corinthians 6:17	I am united with the Lord, and I am one with Him in spirit.
1 Corinthians 6:19–20	I have been bought with a price and I belong to God.
1 Corinthians 12:27	I am a member of Christ's body.
Ephesians 1:3–8	I have been chosen by God and adopted as His child.
Colossians 1:13–14	I have been redeemed and forgiven of all my sins.
Colossians 2:9–10	I am complete in Christ.
Hebrews 4:14–16	I have direct access to the throne of grace through Jesus Christ.

I am secure . . .

Romans 8:1–2	I am free from condemnation.
Romans 8:28	I am assured that God works for my good in all circumstances.
Romans 8:31–39	I am free from any condemnation brought against me and I cannot be separated from the love of God.

2 Corinthians 1:21–22	I have been established, anointed, and sealed by God.
Colossians 3:1–4	I am hidden with Christ in God.
Philippians 1:6	I am confident that God will complete the good work He started in me.
Philippians 3:20	I am a citizen of heaven.
2 Timothy 1:7	I have not been given a spirit of fear but of power, love, and a sound mind.
John 5:18	I am born of God, and the evil one cannot touch me.

I am significant . . .

John 15:5	I am a branch of Jesus Christ, the true vine, and a channel of his life.
John 15:16	I have been chosen and appointed to bear fruit.
1 Corinthians 3:16	I am God's temple.
2 Corinthians 5:17–21	I am a minister of reconciliation for God.
Ephesians 2:6	I am seated with Jesus Christ in the heavenly realm.
Ephesians 2:10	I am God's workmanship.
Ephesians 3:12	I may approach God with freedom and confidence.
Philippians 4:13	I can do all things through Christ, who strengthens me.

*The more you reaffirm who you are in Christ,
the more your behavior will begin to reflect your
true identity!*

....

What Matters

It doesn't matter who we were yesterday,
or what we did—it matters that God
wants to do something with our lives today.
—Jan Coates
Author, *Set Free*

....

INSTRUCTIONS

- Cut out the *What Matters* card on dotted lines.
- Laminate it so it will endure.
- Keep it in your billfold as a reminder that God doesn't care about your past, he cares about your present and future.

Questions and Answers About Counseling

Compiled by Dr. Tim Clinton, President,
American Association of Christian
Counselors

Q. *As a survivor of child abuse, how do I know if I need counseling?*

A. If you are unable to manage bad days and distress interferes with normal daily function and enjoyment of life, generally, I would suggest seeking counseling or outside help.

You may be experiencing distress in a number of common ways—depression, anxiety, or anger—and can be increasingly difficult to control. You may also be experiencing post-traumatic stress, or PTSD, remembering fragments, or complete segments, of intrusive and intense memories and nightmares of the trauma. Some survivors experience a "reliving of the abuse." You may also experience other symptoms, including: hyper vigilance, easy-startle reflex, difficulties with thinking and concentration, sleep disturbances, avoidance of people and events that trigger reminders of the abuse, and an overall sense of dread and foreboding about living.

Abuse survivors also may encounter relational problems with other people. You may struggle with marital conflicts, including sexual avoidance and the inability to become aroused or sustain sexual arousal. You may become easily angered or irritable toward certain persons, and may seek to avoid certain people and interpersonal situations that are fraught with conflict or irritation.

Finally, abuse victims may experience spiritual symptoms. You may feel an estrangement from God, lack of zest and vitality in your spiritual life, and a sense of "spiritual deadness" or just "going through the motions." Church can become a struggle, something you often avoid. You may also feel guilt and anger related to spiritual issues.

Q. *Is counseling important to my healing process?*

A. Counseling is often essential to the adult healing of child abuse, especially if you did not experience nurture, support, and love from within your family during and after the trauma. Often, adult survivors of abuse repress symptoms until a crisis in adulthood triggers a flood of unwanted memories, confusion, fear, and anger. Usually a wise and experienced counselor or group can help you sort through and resolve these repressed issues and emotions.

   We believe Christ is the true healing source. He gives child abuse survivors the power to sustain their healing journey through forgiveness, honesty, courage, and maturity. We also believe that the experience of salvation alone—the reception of Christ into one's heart and life—does not bring such healing. The abuse survivor must face the abuse, renounce the evil and put it on the cross, and learn to appropriate God's ever-available power for renewed living.

Q. *What do I look for in a Christian counselor?*

A. Seek out a Christian whose counseling practice or ministry is permeated with his or her faith and Christian life, rather than a Christian who merely does counseling from a secular perspective, without bringing Christ into the counseling effort. With your consent and invitation, such a counselor willingly prays with you, will use Scripture in session, will refer to Scriptural principles, and will encourage change that incorporates spiritual disciplines and principles of various kinds. This counselor should not impose or pressure you with the things of Christ, but should be adept at listen-

needs and adapting the things of faith to your needs, and with your consent.

If you are seeking help from a professional therapist—psychologist, social worker, professional counselor, or marriage and family therapist—he or she should be duly licensed by the state, have an impeccable ethical record, and be able to give a number of solid references attesting to his or her excellence and ethics. Keep in mind that abused women tend to work better with other women in the beginning stages of counseling. Then they may work best with men as they work primarily to resolve issues around a male abuser.

You may also receive effective help from church-based recovery groups, led by an experienced lay counselor or a healing survivor.

Q. *What can I expect from counseling?*

A. Counseling, in the end, should leave you in a better place than when you began the journey. In other words, you should be living more good days than bad ones. Unfortunately, unlike the computer, our minds don't have a "delete" button. Consequently, counseling will not eradicate all your problems; however, over time, counseling should equip you with the tools to manage and control many of the symptoms and problems you face in day-to-day life.

The initial phase of counseling may be somewhat difficult. It can be a time of emotional distress, involving an honest assessment of situations you thought you had resolved (and probably had learned to effectively avoid and suppress). Your counselor should give you a realistic hope for change and a fairly clear plan for accomplishing some agreed-upon goals within a reasonable time frame. Expect, even demand, that your counselor give you a reasonable time for concluding counseling. It should not go on interminably.

Some counselors will expect you to do the bulk of the work outside sessions in the form of homework, which he or she monitors and adjusts with each visit. Others will do most of the work with you in session. Still others will mix in-session work with homework. Each counselor is different in this regard, and you need to find a way of working on your issues that best meets your needs and abilities. Expect your counselor to assess and build on your strengths and what has worked for you, if only partially, in the past.

Most important, expect your counselor to keep your needs and interests paramount in all the work you do together. Counselors who talk excessively about themselves or other patients, requiring conformation to their model of counseling, or demonstrating behavior that suggests their needs are more important than yours, are no good for you.

Q. *Where can I go for help?*

A. The Resource Guide located in Appendix D provides an extensive list of counselors, support groups, online spiritual help, and emergency contacts. In addition, I would recommend the American Association of Christian Counselors (AACC), of which I am the president.

AACC provides a Counselor Care Network, representing fifty thousand Christian counseling professionals, pastors, and lay helpers, actively serving all fifty states, as well as fifty international locations. AACC offers support, insight, encouragement, and fellowship, and is uniquely poised to keep its members informed of the most recent developments, trends, and challenges in the field of Christian counseling. AACC members are equipped with biblically sound resources and psychologically accurate methods to help them be effective caregivers.

APPENDIX D

Resource Guide[1]

COUNSELING AND THERAPY

American Association of Christian Counselors (AACC)
P.O. Box 739   434-525-9470
Forest, VA 24551   *www.aacc.net*
1-800-526-8673

Counseling, Therapy
    (National database listing nearly fifty thousand licensed professionals, pastors, and lay counselors. Nationwide Counselor Care Network with member services in fifty nations. AACC offers nondenominational, biblically sound, and psychologically accurate services. Continuing education, graduate-level training, clinical and consulting services, and benefits for professional and pastoral caregivers in both traditional and distance formats.)

American Association of Pastoral Counselors (AAPC)
9504-A Lee Highway   703-385-6967
Fairfax, VA 22031-2303   *www.aapc.org*

Pastoral Counseling
    (National database listing thirty-two hundred individual AAPC members.)

---

[1]The organizations listed are intended as suggestions to assist you in finding help. The listings are not an endorsement. All information furnished by organization and/or its Web site.

Christian Counselors Directory
www.christiantherapist.com

Counseling, Therapy
(National database with over one thousand Christian counselors and mental health clinics in over six hundred communities.)

Meier Clinics
2100 Manchester Rd.,   1-888-7CLINIC
Ste. 1510   *www.meierclinics.com* .
Wheaton, IL 60187-4561

Counseling, Therapy
(Twenty-two locations throughout the U.S. Professional
team of psychiatrists, psychologists, social workers, family counselors, and pastoral counselors providing hope and healing for
the mind, body, and spirit. Offers outpatient, intensive outpatient, day program, and e-therapy.)

New Life Ministries
P.O. Box 866997   1-800-NEW-LIFE
Plano, TX 75086   *www.newlife.com*
1-800-639-5433

Counseling, Therapy
(Referral service and national database, offering biblically
based counseling network in sixteen states with over five hundred Christian counselors. Licensed professional therapists
counsel from a nondenominational Christian perspective. Focus
is to minister spiritually, emotionally, and physically.)

RAPHA
1-800-383-HOPE   *www.rapha.info*
1-877-257-0449

Counseling, Therapy
(Integrates Scripture and the love of Jesus Christ to provide

Christ-centered psychiatric treatment and professional counseling that focuses on the physical, psychological, and spiritual dimensions of a person in need.)

RESOURCE GUIDE
RECOVERY AND SUPPORT

Alcoholics Victorious
www.alcoholicsvictorious.org

Ministry and Support Group Database, Christian Support Groups, Twelve-Step Support Groups, Self-Help Clearinghouses
(Over fifteen hundred local Christian support groups listed in database.)

Association of Gospel Rescue Missions
1045 Swift   e-mail: agrm@agrm.org
Kansas City, MO 64116   *www.rescuemissions.org*
1-800-4RESCUE

Rehabilitation, education, biblical counseling, work training, family services, and other resources to help overcome life controlling issues.
(More than three hundred rescue missions in communities across North America. In addition to rehabilitation and job training, many rescue missions offer parenting classes, counseling for abuse survivors, work therapy, and computer education. In most cases, individuals can receive necessary care without having to be separated from their children.)

Celebrate Recovery
One Saddleback Parkway   *www.celebraterecovery.com*
Lake Forest, CA 92630

Ministry and Support Groups
Saddleback Church's Christ-centered Celebrate Recovery ministry, based on "8 Recovery Principles."
(Online search engine lists local groups.)

Christian Recovery International
Dale S. Ryan   *www.christianrecovery.com*
Christian Recovery
International
P.O. Box 215
Brea, CA 92822

Ministry and Support Groups
(A coalition of ministries dedicated to helping the Christian community become a safe and helpful place for people recovering from addiction, abuse, or trauma.)

Christians in Recovery
P.O. Box 4422   *www.christians-in*
Tequesta, FL 33469   *recovery.org*

Ministry and Support Groups
Recovery support tools and resources.
Chat room, message board, online meetings, groups, and newsletters.
(Over one thousand informational pages and resources for people in recovery from abuse, dysfunctional behaviors, and addictions. National, searchable database for organizations, ministries, recovery groups, meetings, counselors, etc.)

Overcomers Outreach
P.O. Box 2208   *info.overcomersoutreach.org*
Oakhurst, CA 93644   *www.overcomersoutreach.org*
1-800-310-3001

Ministry and Support Groups
Provides a two-way bridge between traditional Twelve-Step support groups and people within churches of all denominations, utilizing the twelve steps of Alcoholics Anonymous along with Scriptures.
Individuals reluctant to attend recovery groups in the community can come to Christ-centered Overcomers Outreach

groups and find a safe place to share through the rule of anonymity.

(One thousand support groups. Receives referrals from Focus on the Family, The Billy Graham Evangelistic Association, The 700 Club, treatment centers, churches, hospitals, prisons, pastors, and therapists.)

The Salvation Army
The Salvation Army   703-684-5500
615 Slaters Lane   *www.salvationarmy.org*
P.O. Box 269   *www.salvationarmyusa.org*
Alexandria, VA 22313-
0269

Ministry, support groups, counseling, shelter, outreach, educational and sports programs, church. Colleges, secondary schools, child day care, hospitals, homeless shelters, addiction rehabilitation centers, and emergency material assistance programs are also available.

(Religious and social service activities serve nearly one hundred million people annually in 109 countries. Worldwide locations. Online search engine to local services plus listings in most Yellow Pages.)

RESOURCE GUIDE
ONLINE EVANGELISM AND SPIRITUAL GROWTH

Back to the Bible
www.backtothebible.org

Radio, TV, the Internet, and other media share the Gospel message and help Christians grow to spiritual maturity. With broadcasts in more than twenty-five languages and an Internet reach to millions, Back to the Bible teaches the Word and touches the world.

Billy Graham Evangelistic Association
www.billygraham.org

Daily Scripture, spiritual help, articles, devotionals, radio, prayer, magazine, crusades, and training.

Christian Answers
www.christiananswers.net

Biblical answers to contemporary questions.

Christian Survivors Ministries
www.christiansurvivors.com

Active community for child abuse survivors, centered around moderated message board and forums. Journaling workshops, articles, Scripture.

Christianity Today International
www.todayschristian   *www.christianitytoday.com*
woman.com

Inspirational articles, community message board, magazine, spiritual help, Scripture, women's ministry, church locator, and more.

Crosswalk
www.crosswalk.com

Built around four primary content areas—Faith, Family, Fun, and Community. Each category is further subdivided into areas of significance to many Christians, including Bible study, devotionals, marriage, parenting, music, etc.

Focus on the Family
www.family.org   *www.troubledwith.com*

Publications and on-site resources that affect the family in any way. Husband-wife relationships, parenting, teens, juveniles, and small children are addressed in a professional way and from a biblical perspective.

The Gideons International
www.gideons.org

Includes Bible helps and Bible distribution services.

(Serves as extended missionary arm of the church. Members place and distribute Scriptures in 179 countries in eighty-two languages.)

Gospel Communications
www.gospelcom.net

Women's Bible studies, devotionals, newsletters, support, shopping, and more.

(*Gospelcom.net* includes three hundred individual online ministries working to use technology and the Internet to reach the world with the message of Jesus Christ.)

Prison Fellowship Ministries
www.pfm.org

Radio commentary, daily Scripture, inspirational articles, magazine, news, search program to local offices, in-prison Bible studies, newspaper, seminars, and evangelism.

(Ministers to prisoners, ex-prisoners, and their families, including the children.)

Women of Faith
www.womenoffaith.com

Provides inspiration articles, community message board, and conferences.

Please consider a local church as a rich resource for worship, praise, fellowship, Bible study, women's ministry, and community support. To find a church, try your Yellow Pages, ask a friend or co-worker, or check your local newspaper for church listings. You may also perform an Internet search using "church locator."

RESOURCE GUIDE
EMERGENCY SERVICES

Public Emergency
911

Local emergency telephone assistance
(To save a life, report a fire, or stop a crime, call 9-1-1. For non-emergencies, use the police, fire, and medical service telephone numbers provided in the white pages of the local phone book.)

Childhelp USA®
1-800-422-4453   *www.childhelpusa.org*
1-800-792-5200

National Child Abuse Hotline
(National resource with local referral networks. Hotline offers multilingual crisis intervention, information, literature, and referrals. State-of-the-art technology provides translators in nearly 140 languages.)

Department of Social Services
1-800-342-3720   *www.os.dhhs.gov*

Hotline
(National resource with local referral networks. Hotline offers multilingual crisis intervention, information, literature, and referrals. State-of-the-art technology provides translators in nearly 140 languages.)

Girls and Boys Town
1-800-448-3000   *www.girlsandboystown.org*

Hotline
(Crisis, resource, and referral line. For children and parents

in any type of personal crisis. Accredited by the American Association of Suicidology.)

National Domestic Violence
   1-800-799-7233   *www.ndvh.org*

   Hotline
      (National resource with local referral networks. Hotline offers multilingual crisis intervention, information, literature, and referrals. State-of-the-art technology provides translators in nearly 140 languages.)

Suicide Help
   1-800-SUICIDE   *www.suicidehotlines.com*

   Hotline
      (Help get you through the moment so that you can live another day—so that your cure will be able to save you.)

Suicide Prevention
   1-888-248-2587

   Hotline

Rape, Abuse, and Incest National Network (RAINN)
   1-800-656-HOPE   *www.rainn.org*

   Hotline
      (Nation's largest anti–sexual assault organization with over one thousand affiliates.)

National Runaway Hotline/National Runaway Foundation
   1-800-621-4000   *www.nrscrisisline.org*
   1-800-231-6946

   Hotline
      (Provides crisis intervention and travel assistance to runaways. National shelter referral. Message relay services to set up

conference calls to parent at the request of the child. Database includes over thirty thousand shelters and organizations.)

Covenant House—Nineline
1-800-999-9999 *www.covenanthouse.org/ nineline/kid*

Hotline
(Crisis line for youth, teens, and families. National outreach with local referrals for youth and parents regarding drugs, abuse, homelessness, runaway children, and message relays.)

Kids Save
1-800-8KID-123 *www.kidspeace.org/*
1-800-334-4KID

Hotline
Helps parents, caregivers, and professionals caring for children and adults with disabilities, terminal illnesses, or those at risk of abuse or neglect.
(Offers referrals to shelters, mental health services, safe centers for sexual abuse, substance abuse, family counseling, residential care, adoption/foster care, and more.)

Please Note: Most services listed in "Emergency Services" section offer free and confidential hotlines, available 24 hours a day/7 days a week.

Steps to Peace With God

STEP 1

- God's Purpose: Peace and Life
  God loves you and wants you to experience peace and
  life—abundant and eternal.
- The Bible says . . .
  "We have peace with God through our Lord Jesus
  Christ" (Romans 5:1b).
  "For God so loved the world that he gave his one and
  only Son, that whoever believes in him shall not perish but
  have everlasting life" (John 3:16).
  "I have come that they may have life, and have it to the
  full" (John 10:10).
  Why don't most people have this peace and abundant
  life that God planned for us to have?

STEP 2

- The Problem: Our Separation
  God created us in his own image to have an abundant
  life. He did not make us as robots, to automatically love
  and obey him. God gave us a will and a freedom of choice.
  We chose to disobey God and go our own willful way.
  We still make this choice today. This results in separation
  from God.
- The Bible says . . .

"For all have sinned and fall short of the glory of God" (Romans 3:23).

"For the wages of sin is death, but the gift of God is eternal life in Christ Jesus our Lord" (Romans 6:23).

- Our Attempts to Reach God

    People have tried in many ways to bridge this gap between themselves and God.

- The Bible says . . .

    "There is a way that seems right to a man, but in the end it leads to death" (Proverbs 14:12).

    "But your iniquities have separated you from your God; your sins have hidden his face from you, so that he will not hear" (Isaiah 59:2).

    No bridge reaches God . . . except one.

STEP 3

- God's Bridge: The Cross

    Jesus Christ died on the cross and rose from the grave. He paid the penalty for our sin and bridged the gap between God and people.

- The Bible says . . .

    "For there is one God and one mediator between God and men, the man Christ Jesus" (1 Timothy 2:5).

    "For Christ died for sins once for all, the righteous for the unrighteous, to bring you to God" (1 Peter 3:18).

    "But God demonstrates his own love for us in this: While we were still sinners, Christ died for us" (Romans 5:8).

    God has provided the only way. Each person must make a choice.

STEP 4

- Our Response: Receive Christ

    We must trust Jesus Christ as Lord and Savior and receive him by personal invitation.

- The Bible says . . .

   "Here I am! I stand at the door and knock. If anyone hears my voice and opens the door, I will come in and eat with him, and he with me" (Revelation 3:20).

   "Yet to all who received him, to those who believed in his name, he gave the right to become children of God" (John 1:12).

   "That if you confess with your mouth, 'Jesus is Lord,' and believe in your heart that God raised him from the dead, you will be saved" (Romans 10:9).

- Where are you?

   Will you receive Jesus Christ right now?

   Here is how you can receive Christ:

STEP 5

- How to Pray:

   Dear Lord Jesus, I know that I am a sinner and need your forgiveness. I believe that you died for my sins. I want to turn from my sins. I now invite you to come into my heart and life. I want to trust and follow you as Lord and Savior. In Jesus' name, Amen.

Date _____ Signature _____

- The Bible says . . .

   "Everyone who calls on the name of the Lord will be saved" (Romans 10:13).

Did you sincerely ask Jesus Christ to come into your life? Where is he right now? What has he given you?

   "For it is by grace you have been saved, through faith— and this not from yourselves, it is the gift of God—not by works, so that no one can boast" (Ephesians 2:8–9).

   Receiving Christ, we are born into God's family through the supernatural work of the Holy Spirit who dwells in every believer. This is called regeneration, or the "new birth."

This is just the beginning of a wonderful new life in Christ. To deepen this relationship you should:

1. Read your Bible every day to know Christ better.
2. Talk to God in prayer every day.
3. Tell others about Christ.
4. Worship, fellowship, and serve with other Christians in a church where Christ is preached.
5. As Christ's representative in a needy world, demonstrate your new life by your love and concern for others.

Facts About Child Abuse in the United States

STATISTICS

- Every two minutes a child is sexually assaulted.
- Sixty-three percent increase in reported child abuse over the last ten years.
- Fifty million women in the U.S., or one in three, were abused as children.
- Two children die daily in the U.S. at the hands of an abuser.

TOTAL ANNUAL COST

Hospitalization	$6,205,395,000
Chronic Health Problems	2,987,957,400
Mental Health Care System	425,110,400
Child Welfare System	14,400,000,000
Law Enforcement	24,709,800
Judicial System	341,174,701
Total Direct Costs	$24,384,347,302

HIDDEN CONSEQUENCES AND LONG-TERM OUTCOMES OF CHILD MALTREATMENT

- *Physical and Mental*

  Brain injuries: dysfunction, contusions, intracranial and

intraocular hemorrhages, atrophy, and changes in the part of the brain linked to memory, emotions, and basic drives.

Disease: child and adolescent sexual abuse is associated with the risk of sexually transmitted diseases, including HIV, gonorrhea, and syphilis.

Disability: abuse and neglect are associated with neuromotor handicaps, physical defects, growth and mental retardation, and speech problems.

Mental health disorders: maltreated children tend to have heightened levels of depression, hopelessness, and low self-esteem. A recent Kaiser Permanente indicates 67 percent of females with mental health disorders were abused as children.

- *Cognitive and Educational*

    Disorders: language deficits, reduced cognitive functioning, and attention deficit disorders.

- *Social and Behavioral*

    Antisocial behavior, self-destructiveness, and physical aggression.
    Difficulty developing stable attachments; problems developing relationships and trust.

    Child sexual abuse is a risk factor for adolescent pregnancy.

    Increased risk for substance abuse:
    Eighty percent of substance abusers were abused as children.
    Eighty to ninety percent of recovery and outreach ministry residents were abused as children.

    Increased risk for incarceration:
    Eighty percent of prison population were abused as children.
    Ninety-five percent of prostitutes were sexually abused as children.

Ninety-three percent of female prison inmates were
abused as children.

Sources:
   www.prevent-abuse-now.com/stats
   www.preventchildabuse.org
   www.childtrends.org
   www.washtimes.com
   www.safechild.org/abuse.htm

ENDNOTES

CHAPTER ONE
1. http://www.godswork.org/enpoem42.htm
   http://my.homewithgod.com/lanell/TheChosen-
   Vessel.html
   http://www.godswork.org/emailmessage7.htm
   http://www.gladness.com/modules.php?name=Content&
   pa=showpage&pid=43

CHAPTER THREE
1. www.shema.com; www.Ldolphin.org; www.forerunner.com

CHAPTER FOUR
1. Lynn Heitritter and Jeanette Vought, *Helping Victims of
   Sexual Abuse* (Bloomington, MN: Bethany House Publishers, 1989), 44.
2. E. M. Bounds, "Prayer and Faith," in *E. M. Bounds on
   Prayer*, (New Kensington, PA: Whitaker House, 1997),
   108.

CHAPTER FIVE
1. A. W. Tozer, *Tozer Topical Reader*, comp. Ron Eggert
   (Camp Hill, PA, Christian Publications, 1998), 2.185.
2. Oswald Chambers, "Repentance," in *My Utmost For His
   Highest* (Grand Rapids: Discovery, 1992), "Repentance,"
   Dec. 7.

CHAPTER SEVEN

1. A. W. Tozer, *The Tozer Topical Reader*, comp. Ron Eggert (Camp Hill, PA: Christian Publications, 1998), 2.171.
2. Neil Anderson, *Victory Over Darkness* (Ventura, CA: Regal, 1990), 49.
3.———, *Who I Am in Christ* (Ventura, CA: Regal, 2001, 1993), 278.
4. Dr. Dan B. Allender, *The Wounded Heart* (Colorado Springs: Navpress, 1990), 174.

CHAPTER EIGHT

1. Henry T. Blackaby & Claude V. King, *Experiencing God*, (Nashville: Broadman & Holman, 1994), 2.
2. Martin Smith, "God Is a Conversation," in *The Word Is Very Near You*, (Cambridge: Cowley, 1989), 20–21.

CHAPTER ELEVEN

1. Safe Child Program Child Abuse Page. http://www.safechild.org/abuse.htm.

APPENDIX A

1. Henry T. Blackaby and Claude V. King, *Experiencing God: Knowing and Doing the Will of God* (Nashville, TN: Lifeway), 220–221.

BIBLIOGRAPHY

Anderson, Neil T. *The Bondage Breaker*. Eugene, OR: Harvest House, 2000.

Anderson, Neil T. *Victory Over the Darkness*. Ventura, CA: Regal Books, 1990, 2000.

Blackaby, Henry T. and Claude V. King. *Experiencing God*. Nashville, TN: Broadman & Holman, 1994.

———*Experiencing God: Knowing and Doing the Will of God*. Nashville, TN: LifeWay, 1990.

Chalk, Rosemary; Alison Gibbons; and Harriet J. Scarupa. "The Multiple Dimensions of Child Abuse and Neglect: New Insights into an Old Problem." *Trends Child Research Brief*, May 2002, www.childtrends.org/files/childabuserb.pdf.

"Child Abuse and Neglect Statistics," The National Committee to Prevent Child Abuse, April, 1995, www.prevent-abuse-now.com/stats.html.

Fromm, Suzette. "Total Estimated Cost of Child Abuse and Neglect in the United States." Statistical Evidence, 2001, Prevent Child Abuse America. www.preventchildabuse.org/learn_more/research_docs/cost_analysis.pdf.

Frangipane, Francis. *The River of Life*. New Kensington, PA: Whitaker, 1993.

Heitritter, Lynn, and Jeanette Vought. *Helping Victims of Sexual Abuse*. Bloomington, MN: Bethany House Publishers, 1989.

Kraizer, Sherryll, Ph.D. "The Problem." Safe Child Program,

Coalition for Children, Inc., www.safechild.org/ abuse.htm.

Life Application Study Bible. Wheaton, IL: Tyndale, 1988, 1989, 1990, 1991, 1993, 1996.

Mullen, Paul E., and Jillian Fleming. "Long-term Effects of Child Sexual Abuse." *Issues in Child Abuse Prevention*, Number 9, Autumn 1998, www.aifs.org.au/nch/ issues9.html.

Murray, Andrew. *Abide in Christ*. Fort Washington, PA: Christian Literature Crusade, 1997.

Nouwen, Henri J.M. *The Wounded Healer*. New York, NY: Image, Doubleday, 1979.

Peterson, Eugene H. *The Message: The New Testament, Psalms and Proverbs*, Colorado Springs, CO: Navpress, 1993, 1994, 1995.

———.*The Message: The Old Testament Prophets*. Colorado Springs, CO: Navpress, 2000.

Snell, Tracy L. "Bureau of Justice Statistics Bulletin, Women in Prison." NCJ–145321, March 1994, www.ojp. usdoj.gov/bjs/pub/ascii/wopris.txt.html.

Stanley, Charles. *The Blessings of Brokenness*. Grand Rapids, MI: Zondervan, 1997.

The NIV *Study Bible*. Grand Rapids, MI: Zondervan, 1985.

Tozer, A.W. *The Pursuit of God*. Camp Hill, PA: Christian Publications, 1982, 1993.

———.*The Tozer Topical Reader*. Compiled by Ron Eggert. Camp Hill, PA: Christian Publications, Volume 1–2, 1998.

Woznicki, Katrina, "Child abuse causes lasting health effects." *The Washington Times*, June 13, 2002, www.washtimes.com. www.survivorshealingcenter.org.html.

Zodhiates, Spiros. *The Complete Word Study Dictionary, New Testament*. Chattanooga, TN: AMC, 1993.

———.*The Complete Word Study New Testament, KJV*. Chattanooga, TN: AMC, 1991, 1992.

———.*The Complete Word Study Old Testament, KJV*. Chattanooga, TN: AMC, 1994.